A Kinder Voice

A Kinder Voice

Releasing Your Inner Critics
with Mindfulness Slogans

Thérèse Jacobs-Stewart

Hazelden
Publishing

Hazelden Publishing
Center City, Minnesota 55012
hazelden.org/bookstore

Library of Congress Cataloging-in-Publication Data

Names: Jacobs-Stewart, Thérèse, author.
Title: A kinder voice : releasing your inner critics with mindfulness
    slogans / Thérèse Jacobs-Stewart.
Description: Center City, Minnesota : Hazelden Publishing, [2016] |
    Includes bibliographical references.
Identifiers: LCCN 2016010549 | ISBN 9781616496395 (softcover)
Subjects: LCSH: Meditation. | Peace of mind. | Peace of mind—
    Religious aspects. | Criticism, Personal.
Classification: LCC BL627 .J33 2016 | DDC 158.1/2—dc23
LC record available at https://lccn.loc.gov/2016010549

Editor's note
The stories in the book are based on actual experiences. The names and
some details may have been changed to protect the privacy of those mentioned in this publication.

This publication is not intended as a substitute for the advice of health
care professionals.

Readers should be aware that websites listed in this work may have
changed or disappeared between when this book was written and when
it is read.

Alcoholics Anonymous, AA, and the Big Book are registered trade-
marks of Alcoholics Anonymous World Services, Inc.

20 19 18 17 16   1 2 3 4 5 6

Interior design: Terri Kinne

May you feel safe,
May you be happy,
May you be healthy,
May you live with ease.[1]

Contents

Acknowledgments

To Zoketsu Norman Fischer, whose writings on compassion training and meditation have inspired this book. Thank you, roshi, for your teaching.

To Doug Toft, bodhisattva-brother and fellow writer. Thank you for your support and skill.

To my editor, Sid Farrar. Thank you for your vision.

To my beloved Jim. Thank you for your love and wisdom, and teaching me a kinder voice.

May any merit of this work be of benefit to all beings.

Always Train with Slogans

I have a whole gang of inner critics. Let me tell you about just two of them.

The first one I call *Old Joe* after my dad (dá) because this voice drills like an army master sergeant. Irish to the bone, my dá was red-haired, freckled, and fierce before he turned gray in his early thirties. (Just like me.) He fought Mussolini from the foxholes in North Africa during World War II and never lost the edge of drill sergeant in his voice. He gave us orders and dressed us down if we were birdbrained. Old Joe's voice says, "What have you got between those ears? Sawdust?" Other times this voice belittles people: "Well, those shoes didn't walk themselves over there in front of the TV, now did they?"

The thing is, my dá Joe was raised by *his* dá, who grew up in the old country. Shaming, biting humor was the rule in those days, and a blackthorn shillelagh hung on the wall—an easy reach to whack a sassy child. People in the village of Newton-Stewart called my grandá "Big Red." With flaming hair and fiery temper, he was a force.

Grandá got into trouble with the law because of getting pissed with drink and vandalizing graves, which are sacred to the Irish. He fled the old country and went on to a new life in the New Land. But, his legacy lives on and that voice is inside me now.

Another of my gang of inner critics is *Ms. Perfectionist.* She notices every detail and sees when something is out of place. She spends hours with foil wrappings and bright ribbons making Christmas packages into mini-works-of-art. My mother was like that, and she nearly had a nervous breakdown over it. Although she had four kids, each only a few years apart and me the second born, she tried to make everything just so.

My Grandma Ceil did the same. You could eat off Grandma Ceil's floor, and she was proud of it. Mother said that Grandma spent more time cleaning than talking to her, and I don't think she liked Grandma very much.

I liked Grandma Ceil, though. She gave me dollar bills to put in my pocket. When I stayed at her house, we'd eat dinner on TV trays and have ice cream with chocolate sauce. I liked her spotless, shiny floors and the scent of lemon wax in her house.

My mother lost her eyesight in her eighties and then she lost her memory from dementia. When I brought gifts to her nursing home, they were always wrapped nicely. Mother once said, "I don't know how you got to be such a perfectionist." I laughed because she must have forgotten what she used to be like.

Now I have Grandma Ceil's voice inside me, and I've noticed she can be quite demanding. One of the downsides of perfectionism is that nothing is ever good enough. Once before a family holiday, for instance, I didn't wash and wax the kitchen floor on purpose. It was my ode to imperfection. But, it just about killed me.

What's in This Book for You

This is a book about releasing your inner critics—plural—not by killing them off but rather by first befriending each of them and loving yourself *just the way you are* in the here and now. The practices of mindfulness and loving-kindness meditation offer you ways to do this. Both have been profound medicine for my emotional wounds, and this book explains how they can help you, if you wish.

In the pursuit of peace and freedom from my "gang" of inner critics, I've gone through many months of counseling and attended years of Twelve Step recovery groups. The Twelve Step program is a beautiful thing. It saved me from destroying myself with amphetamines before I knew how to live. The programs of Alcoholics Anonymous and Al-Anon hold that addiction and co-dependency are conditions of spiritual bankruptcy. Nearly forty years after my first Twelve Step meeting, I am still convinced they are right. The implication is that the remedy can be found in spiritual practice.

I work professionally as a psychotherapist. I believe in therapy and have devoted much of my adult life to helping people heal. Yet, during these past three decades, I have also practiced contemplative meditation from both East and West traditions. I studied and became certified as a Spiritual Director in the contemplative Christian practices of the Ignation Exercises[1] and trained for years in mindfulness practices, Zen meditation, and Tibetan traditions. I believe in the power of meditation to change the brain and touch places that talk therapy cannot go.

At the age of twenty-four, I went to a monastery called Nada Hermitage[2] in the foothills of Northern Arizona, looking to find peace and learn how to meditate and pray. Maybe the ancestors that still roam those hills in the spirit world found me; maybe I found them by showing up with a fairly open heart. I discovered a path of mindfulness and meditation that has, for the most part, helped me gain freedom by releasing my inner critics. Though they are still present, their power is profoundly diminished. A similar freedom and release can be yours if you are willing to use the suggestions in this book.

The History of Mind-Training with Slogans

This book introduces you to an ancient Tibetan practice called *mind-training (lojong),* which is built upon the foundation of mindfulness meditation. I first learned of this practice while in Nepal at the Thrangu Tashi Choling Monastery. The most celebrated of all the *lojong* texts, *The Root Text of the Seven Points of Training the Mind,* is a collection of practices to transform negative or critical thought patterns into loving-kindness and compassion for self and others. The teaching is based on a list of ancient slogans originally attributed to the Bengali teacher Atisha in the late 900s.[3]

Yes, *slogans.* In mind-training, pithy ditties—"humorous aphorisms"[4]—inform our spiritual practice and become the object of our contemplation. Over the years, I have returned time and time again to these provocative, memorable slogans. Few other meditations have as deeply touched the shadowy corners of my psyche. I find them uncanny in their power to transform the heart-mind. Mind-training with slogans can rewire your mental habits over time and soften the harsh, strident, and seemingly intractable voices of your inner critics.

To put mind-training with slogans in context, remember that almost all spiritual traditions work with phrases and offer practices in contemplation and mental recitation: saying the rosary, repeating a psalm aloud, reciting a mantra time and again, praying five times a day, or chanting a holy text while on one's knees. The venerable Norman Fischer-roshi,[5] one of the leading experts in bringing *lojong* practice to the West, says, "Working with phrases is an ancient technique for mind training in almost all literature cultures. In serious Jewish, Muslim, and Christian practice, as well as many versions of Buddhism, texts are chanted daily. They are also studied, memorized, and used as sacred instruction to shape and illuminate conduct and thought."[6]

Why have such practices remained relevant for all these centuries? Perhaps the story of Atisha himself and his follower Chekawa can shed light on this question.

Atisha grew up as a fat cat, enjoying the advantages of wealth, royalty, and palace life. But he renounced his riches as a teenager and left on a spiritual sojourn to Sumatra. There he immersed himself in meditation and received instructions in mind-training. Years later, upon his return to India, Atisha reestablished this once-lost teaching.

After Atisha's time, mind-training was guarded as a closely held secret and transmitted only to an inner circle of disciples. These practices were not even written down until several hundred years after Atisha's death, and they did not become widely known until they were later summarized by Chekawa.

Chekawa worked with lepers in India and Tibet and instructed them in mind-training, hoping it would alleviate their suffering. Legend has it that many were subsequently cured of their disease. Due to these tales, mind-training meditations are sometimes referred to as "the dharma for leprosy" in Tibet.

The story gets more interesting, still. One fable has it that Chekawa took his brother with him when he went to teach at a leper colony in Sri Lanka. According to the lore, Chekawa's brother was an incorrigible troublemaker. No one else wanted this good-for-nothing person around. Once at the colony, in fact, Chekawa's brother disrupted the meditation class many times. Eventually he was expelled and relegated to sweeping the halls.

Yet even Chekawa's ne'er-do-well brother noticed that many of the lepers in Chekawa's class attained a certain joy and peace of mind. His curiosity was piqued. He began to sneak to the back of the hall and quietly listen to Chekawa's lectures through a crack in the door. To the amazement of all, Chekawa's brother, too, became kinder and more peaceful.

Chekawa noticed that these teachings seemed to benefit someone who formerly had no interest in meditation. He decided to make the texts more widely available and disseminate mind-training to all who were interested. The secret teachings were no longer a mystery, belonging to a fortunate few.

My thanks, therefore, to Chekawa's brother, who remains unnamed. If the mind-training teachings could benefit him, I figured they could benefit even me. If there was hope for him to gain inner peacefulness, then it is possible for us all.

Mind-Training with Slogans—The Twelve Step Tradition

As the heart of mind-training, slogan practice[7] is also present in our Western culture. Slogans have been a mainstay for people in recovery, who are often surprised by how these pithy sayings can transform a thought or inform a choice.

Ask anyone active in a Twelve Step recovery program: Having a bad day? Up comes "Easy does it."

Worrying about the future? "One day at a time" presents itself.

"Live and let live"—a slogan that even found its way into popular song—can help us refrain from judging other people or demanding that they agree with us.

When faced with a dilemma, members of Al-Anon can say, "Responsible for the effort, not the outcome."

The Serenity Prayer is relevant here, too.[8]

> *God, grant me the serenity*
> *to accept the things I cannot change,*
> *courage to change the things I can,*
> *and wisdom to know the difference.*

This prayer is recited aloud at the end of nearly every Twelve Step meeting, held in the mind by people in recovery in their morning prayers and meditation, and used as a guiding philosophy in the midst of a dilemma. As a result, the prayer becomes rooted in the inner mind, spontaneously popping up in the middle of a stressful situation or sleepless night.

Refrains such as these can take root in our unconscious and arise to elucidate the present moment with a kernel of wisdom. In addition to inspiring us, these persistent and sometimes pesky slogans can even redirect a habituated reaction.

With slogan practice, then, we participate in a wisdom tradition going back many generations in the Twelve Step tradition and more than 2,500 years in the Buddhist lineage—back to the time of Chekawa, Atisha, and the Buddha himself. The teachings on mind-training that have been practiced by Tibetan Buddhists for centuries are now available to you and me as well. Together we can practice them to release our critic-demons and make kinder mental habits our new default setting.

How to Work with Slogans

When we practice with slogans, *repetition is the key.* It takes repetition to develop new neural pathways in the brain. New ways of working with our self-critical thoughts through meditation must be practiced consistently over time. We contemplate, ponder on, and hold slogans in our mind time and again so that they stick, allowing the brain to change in a permanent way.

Research shows that repetition calms the mind by reducing

neural activity in the area of the brain that's involved in self-critical thinking. Repetition enhances learning and creates memory traces in our gray matter. This is why the ancients recommended repetition, repetition, repetition. It works. The road to change is that simple and that fundamental, and we have to *practice* with our whole heart.

As you repeat a slogan, recite it slowly and contemplate one word at a time. Time and again, roll the slogan in your mind. Reflect on its meaning. Hold its wisdom as freedom from your inner critics and contemplate its application in your life.

For further guidance, let's turn to the work of Zen priest Norman Fischer, author of *Training in Compassion: Zen Teachings on the Practice of Lojong.* He offers a Zen-inflected method of working with a slogan, which is to copy it again and again in a notebook and repeat it silently during meditation.

"I stay with the slogan until all of my ideas about it become boring and there is only the slogan itself, like a good wise friend, urging me on," Fischer-roshi says.[9] When you practice like this, the slogan will start to pop into your mind unbidden, a substitute for the many other mindless self-critical or other-critical thoughts that would otherwise be popping up. In this way, the slogan becomes an indispensable tool, coming to your assistance not just when you feel "spiritual" but when you feel stuck in the midst of daily life.

Although formal mind-training practice has fifty-nine slogans, we will be working with only six in this book—a choice few. That's plenty. The entire repertoire of slogans offers us a lifetime of practice, and this book is intended simply to get you started, and perhaps "hooked," on the simplicity, humor, and power of mind-training practice. I hope that these six slogans will steep in your mind and inspire an appetite for more.

If you study and memorize the slogans, you will find that they "arise effortlessly in your mind at the oddest times. They have a haunting quality, and in their recurrence, they can lead you gradually to a more and more subtle understanding of the nature of kindness and compassion."[10] They are the basis for developing a kinder voice.

How to Meditate with a Mindfulness Slogan[11]

1. **Fix the slogan in your mind:**
   - Sit upright on a chair or your meditation cushion.
   - Quiet the body with breath and body awareness.
   - Write the slogan down on a card by your meditation seat.
   - Repeat the slogan silently to yourself again and again.
   - Breathe in the slogan with the inhale; breathe it out with the exhale.

2. **Contemplate with the slogan:**
   - Memorize the slogan.
   - Write down the slogan in your journal (suggested: 108 times!).
   - As with a mantra, turn the slogan in your mind again and again, soaking in the words.

3. **Discuss the meaning of the slogan with others:**

   ■ Reflect on the slogan.

   ■ Talk about the slogan with your friends.

   ■ Read commentary on the slogan.

4. **Carry the slogan in your awareness as you go through your week:**

   ■ Develop your relationship with the slogan as "an almost physical object, a feeling in the belly or heart."[12]

   ■ Hold the slogan in your mind as you go about your day. Breathe with it, repeat it silently to yourself, and let your inner mind absorb the phrase. This will anchor the slogan more deeply into the heart and body, beyond a simply intellectual grasp.

   ■ When you are walking or driving or cooking or standing in line at the grocery store, or anytime you remember, repeat the slogan in your mind.

   ■ As Norman Fischer-roshi suggests, keep your work with slogans "disciplined but lively. Be serious, attentive, and flexible"[13] as you practice.

How to Use This Book

Now you have the context for our first slogan, which gives this introduction its subtitle: *Always train with slogans.* That's exactly what this book is about. I want you to discover that the use of mindfulness slogans and meditation as tools for change is not something esoteric or weird. These practices tap abilities we all have or can develop. Relatively simple changes in the way we talk to ourselves can make big differences in our quality of life.

You don't need any background in psychology or meditation to use this book. I invite you to relate to it as a companion and to sit with these mindfulness slogans until they become intimate friends. Like human friends, they may surprise you if you take the time from your hurried life to know them.

In each chapter, I suggest one slogan for you to bring into your meditation practice. Guided meditations based on the slogans are woven throughout. You can read this book through from cover to cover to get the gist. Or, read the book slowly, a chapter or paragraph at a time, reflecting as you go.

Occasionally you will also be greeted by short passages in italics, such as this one:

> *Rest in the openness of mind.*
> *Openness of mind . . .*
> *Opening the mind . . .*

I've inserted these to reinforce key ideas and punctuate the pages with the feeling of slogan practice. If you wish, pause from reading when you see these passages, close your eyes, and turn the phrases over in your mind. Taking such occasional mindfulness breaks can help you understand this text at a deeper level and make the transition from *reading* about the practice to actually *doing* it.

As you go through this book, also return to the places that speak to you, either because you are drawn to a particular slogan or even because a slogan annoys you. In spiritual-direction-speak, we call this "noticing what's juicy." The advice is to stay with a juicy concept, slogan, or meditation. Don't run. Turn toward your reaction. Be curious and explore. Without some juice, meditation is going to sit on the surface and stay purely intellectual. Don't stop there! Dare to reflect deeply and let these ancient slogans unleash their mystical, unbounded power to transform.

However, a word of caution: *This book is not a substitute for professional care, and it is not a treatment for any mental or emotional condition.* Sometimes mindfulness work and meditating with slogans can stir up uncomfortable feelings, especially if you have a history of trauma. Feel free to move on from a particular slogan, discuss it with a friend or sponsor (or counselor), or let it go. It's okay to rest for a while. You can come back to that slogan or practice at another time.

    . . . Always train with slogans . . .

❖

1

Everything Is of the Nature to Change (Even Us)

When I started my career as a psychotherapist, a predominant theory was that each of us has a "happiness set point" determined in childhood. This psychological set point acted as a ceiling on joy, determining how much optimism or satisfaction one could expect in life. Basically, you got what you got and good luck with that, whatever it was.

This theory did not bode well for me. My family of origin had been plagued by alcoholism and depression, violence and fear. I'd come out of my upbringing with a deep sense of shame, feelings of inadequacy, and an addiction to amphetamines in my teens and twenties. I didn't want to be stuck with my family's set point, doomed to struggle with fierce inner critics and a limited capacity to receive care from others.

I felt the limitations of my happiness threshold on nearly a daily basis. One March afternoon it was particularly vivid. By that time, I was clean from amphetamine use and taking the spiritual part of recovery to heart. I had traipsed to the Far East to study meditation and receive instruction at the well-known Thrangu Tashi Choling Monastery in Boudha, Nepal.

I remember a day when tall mountains hugged the valley under an intense sapphire sky and a cacophony of prayer flags flapped outside the temple doors. Inside, the scent of incense and butter lamps was pungent. Guttural chanting scraped the air and cymbals clanged between nerve-racking, bellowing horns. Eastern temples chant and blow and clang to scare away evil spirits, but I wondered if it also had a practical purpose of keeping us all from nodding off.

A young nun with a shaved head and wearing scarlet and yellow robes led the meditation in a singsong voice. She told us to sit in quietude for a few moments and then, in our mind's eye, bring up a picture of someone easy to care about.

Johnny, my handsome Himalayan cat, came to mind first. I could recall his crossed blue eyes and silky white fur, feel the vibration of his purr and the warmth of his body on my lap. I was a little disappointed that a pet cat had come to mind before any of the people in my life, but—oh well—we weren't supposed to censor.

After bringing to mind this "easy-to-care-about" being, we were instructed to send thoughts of kindness and appreciation for their presence in our lives. We were to hold them in gratitude and wish them well-being.

The next twist in the diffident nun's instructions held a surprise. After streaming positive thoughts toward the other, she told us to turn the same energy and intention inward. We were to direct thoughts of well-being and kindness toward ourselves, even holding our own name in mind if we wished.

I could barely stand that meditation. The image that came to me was of a plant that is all dried out and unable to soak in fluids. Water just sits on top because the soil is too hard and dry to absorb the nutrients. That was my heart—too guarded, too afraid to take in loving-kindness toward myself. My inner critics ruled with the words *You are not good enough.* I wasn't yet aware that these words were just a story in my mind and not the truth. I didn't realize there could be a different reality.

The Science of Change—And What It Means for Our Inner Critics

Since that time I spent in Nepal, modern advances in neuroscience have blown the happiness set point theory to smithereens. Recent research indicates that our emotional and mental patterns, including the repeated stories of our inner critics, trace neural pathways in the brain. No wonder our habits feel so difficult to change. We acquire our emotional habits and the thoughts and actions that go with them, beginning in childhood. Each time we run a mental narrative—such as *I'm not cute enough, skinny enough, smart enough, or good enough*—neurons are etching a pathway in the brain. Each time we react in a habitual way, neurons deepen our pathways until they eventually turn into the equivalent of neural highways in the brain.

These highways sometimes feel so strong that we think they are etched into our bones and define who we are. But there is another reality: We can etch new neural pathways vis-à-vis the same process of repetition. As American neurobiologist Carla Shatz said, "When neurons fire together, they wire together."[1] *With new mental activity we can actually create new neural structures.* Just because our patterns have become "wired in" doesn't mean they are forever fixed.

Everything is of the nature to change. Change is one of the most basic truths of the Universe, embracing the earth around us, our minds, our personalities, and the people we know and love. Not only is this truth embodied in the timeless Eastern spiritual teachings about emptiness and impermanence—it is now also documented by modern science.

The adult brain is far more elastic than previously thought. Our brains are in sync with the physical universe—in constant motion. Everything from the unpredictability of quantum particles to the fact that our Sun will one day swell up and swallow our planet tells us that the world is turbulent.

Even the atoms in our very brains don't stay still. As Rick Hanson notes in his book *Buddha's Brain,* "Regions in the PFC [prefrontal cortex] that support consciousness are updated five to eight times a second."[2]

Whoa. Think about what Hanson is saying here. To put his comment in context, think about how often we get notified that our computer operating system or software system has an update available. Or, consider how often we see ads for the latest and greatest model of cell phone. Updating our technology once every ten or twelve months seems like a lot to me. *(What? My electronics are outdated already? It seems like it was just yesterday when I bought my last iPhone!)* And now Hanson suggests that certain parts of our thinking brains are updating every five to eight seconds. Now *that* is impermanence.

What is the implication of this brain research for our work in releasing our inner critics? It means *we can change our brains, even as adults.* We can change our mental and emotional habits. We can rewire our brains for greater happiness. It *feels* like we can't at times, especially when our inner voice is sharp and critical and we want immediate relief. But it isn't true that we are stuck with a happiness set point. We can release our inner critics and expand our capacity for peace.

Meditation Changes Brain Structure

Mindfulness meditation is one of the powerful methods for changing the brain, the mind, and the heart. Richard Davidson, professor of psychology and psychiatry at the University of Wisconsin–Madison, has done extensive research on the effects of mindfulness meditation on the brain. His research involved taking images of the brains of beginning meditators before and after meditation training, as well as measuring the neural activity in the brains of long-term meditators and Buddhist monks. In an amazing conclusion, Davidson says, "Meditation can change the brain and *forever* alter our sense of well-being."[3]

Other neuroscientists concur. Researcher Sara Lazar[4] and her team at Harvard found that meditation is far more than a feel-good, relaxing practice; it actually alters the very structure of the brain. Not only can mindfulness meditation change the brain—results are demonstrated after a *mere eight weeks of meditating just twenty-seven minutes a day.* What a marvelous return on the investment of our time.

In Lazar's study, magnetic resonance (MR) images were taken of participants' brains before and after mindfulness training. These scans were then compared to the brain scans of a control group of non-meditators. It may be worthwhile to note that in this study, the only method of meditation employed was pure mindfulness—nonjudgmental awareness of sensations, feelings, and states of mind.[5]

After eight weeks, the subjects in Lazar's study showed increased gray matter density in the hippocampus (the part of the brain related to learning and memory) and in structures associated with self-awareness, compassion, and introspection. In addition, participants reported reductions in stress that were correlated with decreased gray-matter density in the amygdala (the fight or flight mechanism of the brain), which is known to play an important role in anxiety and stress.[6] Even more differences were found in long-term meditators, especially the older participants in the study. This suggests that meditation might offset age-related cortical thinning.

In summary, the data from the Lazar study provides "the first structural evidence for . . . [brain] plasticity associated with meditation practice."[7] Again, *everything is of the nature to change*—even our brains. People are not just feeling better when they meditate, their brains are actually changing because they are more relaxed. These are not anecdotal stories embroidered with reports of greater peace and serenity. We're talking science here, and maybe we should take heed.

There's more. It's not only that the adult brain can change but also that we can shape *how* we want our brain to change if we practice meditation on a regular basis. Our friend Richard Davidson states: "What we found is that the longtime practitioners showed brain activation on a scale we have never seen before."[8] He says, "We don't really think of happiness as a skill, but everything we've learned about the brain suggests that it's no different than learning to play the violin or learning to engage in a complex sport. If you practice at it, you'll get better at it."[9]

My initial reaction to this research was: *What? I can change? There is no fixed happiness set point?* There was something I could *do,* an actual set of ancient practices that could change the habits of my mind and free myself from the bondage of self. *Sign me up,* I thought. *I will go to the ends of the earth to learn these meditation practices.*

And so I did, as several of the stories in this book reveal.

What Meditation Does for You and Your Brain

Based on Richard Davidson's pioneering research, here are some of the "promises" of meditation practice:[10]

- *You can rewire your brain's structure and functioning.* It may take thousands of hours of meditation and years of practice, but long-term meditators can actually alter the structure of their brains and rewire them for the better. Ongoing meditative practice increases the brain's neuroplasticity—the ability to reorganize itself and create new neural connections.

- ***Your capacity for happiness will expand.*** University of Wisconsin researchers led by Davidson hooked up 256 sensors to the head of a sixty-six-year-old French monk named Matthieu Ricard, an aide to the Dalai Lama. They found that, due to the neuroplasticity of his brain, he had the largest capacity for happiness ever recorded. "Meditation is not just blissing out under a mango tree, but it completely changes your brain and therefore changes what you are," said Dr. Ricard.

- ***Your empathy and compassion will deepen.*** Davidson's research with Tibetan monks found that when the monks did loving-kindness meditations, their brains generated powerful gamma waves, indicating a compassionate state of mind. These findings suggest that empathy can be cultivated by exercising the brain through loving-kindness meditation.

2

Rest in the Openness of Mind

Odors of mud and mold filled the air after two days of spring rains. Gravel in the soggy parking lot crunched as I approached my black sedan, now dusted with emerald tree pollen. The weekend workshop that I led was long but satisfying and the participants were enthusiastic with their feedback. Afternoon light waned on a job well done. Or so it should have been.

Beep, beep to open the car door, and then the voice of an inner critic started in. It ragged at every flaw in my lectures and facilitation, scrutinizing each imperfection, none too small. *You talked too much. You should listen better. You better watch your ego, girl, and not get carried away with yourself. . . .* This time, I noticed the flushing sensation in my face and numbness spreading through my chest.

Ahhh! I know you. The *Underminer*—the familiar, painful belief that I'm not good enough. In a word: shame.

Once upon a time, combing over each less-than-perfect-part-of-everything-I-did was a way of life. I didn't know then that the voice of the Underminer was shame talking and not the truth. I didn't realize that I was living inside a bubble of my habituated thoughts, what Buddhist psychology calls a "constructed reality."

Not until learning about mindfulness and meditation.

When I started meditating, I thought the process would strong-arm my inner critics into submission and *make* my mind be peaceful. I wanted to get rid of my inner critics and make them go away. As a recovering amphetamine addict, I also hoped (without knowing it) that meditation would deliver a new "natural high," a sort of spiritual opiate to quiet my scruples.

Instead, I experienced meditation as an awakening—perhaps one could even say a rude awakening. Rather than becoming lost inside my judging thoughts and beliefs about myself and others, meditation helped me to see my mind in action. This awareness was both uncomfortable as hell and fabulously freeing.

Our Thoughts Filter Our World

Many of us don't realize that the world of our inner critics is comprised of mostly made-up stories. In our mind, the inner critics seem to speak truth. But, mindfulness can counter these influences with *possibly not.* Maybe the inner critics don't have a handle on what's real. Maybe they speak stories that have been internalized from how we were treated growing up or how we are viewed in our current social environment. Or maybe these stories were simply projected onto us from others who are ignorant or lack self-awareness.

Maybe, then, the inner critics hold ideas that have been *learned.* Just *maybe.*

I think of the 1998 movie *The Truman Show* as an apt metaphor. Actor Jim Carrey plays a character named Truman

Burbank, who is unaware that he is living inside a reality television show, broadcast around the clock to billions of people across the globe. Truman has grown up, and lives, in a fake town full of actors, enclosed in a giant dome equipped with high-tech simulations of sun and sky. The special effects department generates the rain and wind. His world looks and feels real.

At first, Truman is blissful in his ignorance. He greets his neighbors, leaves for work with a bounce in his step, and wears an ear-to-ear smile. He is the only one who doesn't know that he lives inside a giant TV studio, the star in a telethon of reality programming. The story unfolds, portraying a series of noteworthy events in Truman's life. But, the crew makes mistakes, tearing open Truman's delusion, and he eventually figures out that his surroundings are staged. Consequently, Truman embarks on a quest to discover the truth about his life and attempts to escape his stage set. In an effort to preserve profits, however, the producer-director throws up obstacles to prevent Truman from leaving. And even more difficult, Truman must confront his own fears of change.[1]

The Truman Show represents the world of our inner minds. In our case, it's most likely not a diabolical media mogul who has constructed the world we see. Nonetheless we live in a bubble of mental perceptions that filter how we view ourselves and the world around us.

One meditation teacher has suggested that we carry around a "portable stage set" that affects how we experience and interpret our life experiences. Is life a tragedy? An irrelevant comedy?

Are you usually the hero? Or, the victim? Is it a case of "different players, same story"? This is the script of our personal stage set, and the formative experiences of our lives are the scriptwriters.

The voices of our inner critics draw from this narrative. Oftentimes, we aren't actually here in life the way it really is. We are in a carefully constructed world, but we think it's real—like Truman Burbank.

One of the most valuable insights I have gained through the practice of meditation is this: *I am often absorbed in a world largely constructed by my thoughts.* And, I usually don't realize it unless I am practicing mindfulness. This is especially true when it comes to the Land of the Inner Critics. They inhabit a realm of shaming, judging, criticizing, and undermining, deeming ourselves and others as wrong or inadequate. Their view is built of constructed reality. In words attributed to Gautama Buddha, "We are what we think . . . with our thoughts we make the world."

Meeting External Reality with an Internal Response

Sometimes people object to the Buddha's observation. *What? Are you kidding? No way—real things happen. And my view of them is right.* However, the Eastern teachings about constructed reality do not deny the real experiences that give rise to happiness or hurt. When a tree falls, it actually hits the ground; this happens in the physical world. And, there truly are acts of unspeakable cruelty that happen to people. They endure war and abuse. They lose their job, can't find a job, or get fired because they are not good enough to "cut it." These are real experiences.

What I'm suggesting here is simply that *we respond to each external event or situation with an interpretation.* And this internal story can greatly compound our suffering or increase our sorrow. Our story can be used to beat ourselves up or create a justification for hatred or harm.

Perhaps you have met people with markedly different views of a similar experience. For example, I have a neighbor who works as an airline pilot. He is often unhappy with his job. He complains that he works long hours, has to be on call after many years of service to the company, and feels unappreciated. He says his schedule is crappy, his duty periods are unreasonable and unsafe, and customers and crew are usually a pain in the neck. He makes a six-figure salary but feels bitter and is counting the days until he can retire.

On the other hand, my husband, Jim, met another pilot while on jury duty a few months back. Jim had to stay in the jury pool for five consecutive days, waiting to be either selected or dismissed. One morning, as a way to pass the time, he started chatting with the young man sitting next to him. The fellow introduced himself: "I'm an airline pilot and I have the best job in the world. I get to fly in the sky, have lots of days off, and make a really decent salary. I see the world and meet many interesting people. You couldn't meet a luckier guy." Turns out he works for the same company as my neighbor.

Again, we meet each external situation with an internal

response. Sometimes our response seeds suffering and sometimes it seeds peace, as in the case of our two pilots. Often we can't control the external event, but we *can* work with our internal response, our story about what's happening and why.

In Buddhist psychology, this phenomenon is called *dependent co-arising*. According to this teaching, nothing is independent and fixed. Rather, each experience is a complex interplay of event and interpretation. We attribute meaning, for better or worse, to what we experience. We explain what's happening through our internal filter. Writing about dependent co-arising, Barbara Hoetsu O'Brien notes that "things are the *way* they are because they are conditioned by other things. You are conditioned by other people and phenomena. Other people and phenomena are conditioned by you"—there is no such thing as an independent, fixed phenomena.[2]

Gautama Buddha said it this way:

When this is, that is.
This arising, that arises.

The way we see and experience life, in short, is a co-arising of what is external and what is internal. We abide in our inner world of thoughts and views and beliefs, all of which have been shaped by our life experiences. And sometimes our views are more objective than at other times.

Inner Critics Distort Our View

Perhaps you review a situation and say to yourself, *Yup, I was at fault; I was wrong to say or do that.* Consequently, you see that amends are called for. At other times, particularly when your inner critics are fierce and shaming, your appraisal may be distorted.

I still vividly recall a counseling session when my therapist told me that my internal perception was not reliable and should not be trusted. "Your internal voice is *stuck* on critic," she said. "You need to adjust how much you believe what your inner critics are saying—as if you lived in a house where the thermostat was jammed and always read 20 degrees warmer than it really was. You'd have to learn to think, 'Oh, it's not really 90 in here, it's actually only 70.' Similarly, your reading of yourself is too harsh; you have to adjust for the distortion."

Our inner critics are often less than objective. But, we have been conditioned to believe their voice. While Buddhism calls this inner world our constructed reality, Western psychology calls it our "narrative identity." This is another term for the script and portable stage set we carry around, interpreting each experience through a filter that we mostly believe is true.

Even modern physics weighs in on our discussion. Richard Conn Henry, professor of physics and astronomy at Johns Hopkins University, says, "A fundamental conclusion of the new physics . . . acknowledges that the observer creates the reality. As observers, we are personally involved with the creation of our own reality. Physicists are being forced to admit that the universe is a 'mental' construction."

What? Is he kidding? How can the Eastern view that nothing is as solid as it seems be true? It is true as Professor Henry concludes: "The significance of this information is for us to wake up. Get over it, and accept the inarguable conclusion. The Universe is immaterial—mental and spiritual. Live, and enjoy."[3]

We also see the notion that reality is largely in the mind in modern philosophy. German philosopher Immanuel Kant is generally considered the person who made the greatest contribution in this area. Building on the work of earlier philosophers, Kant drew a clear distinction between our perception of reality and the actual object of perception. His key insight was that all we ever know are the structures generated in our minds. The world that gives rise to our perception, what he termed "the thing-in-itself," remains forever unknowable. All we can ever know, proposed Kant, is how reality appears to us—the phenomenon of our experience, "that which appears to be."[4]

Challenges to Escaping from Our Stories

Like Truman Burbank, we find that our world of mental construction with its population of inner critics is difficult to escape. Some of the difficulty comes from a variety of external challenges.

If you are a part of a family, workplace, or social system that is invested in your role, you may get pushback if you try to change. Your perfectionism may be rewarded at work, for example, or supported by a boss who is only too happy to have you give up your weekends to get it right or get it done.

Maybe you have a parent who is living out their dreams through you and doesn't want you to be anything less than a star. I had a client whose father didn't talk to him for eleven years because he quit a minor league baseball career. (His father was an athlete who aspired but never made it into professional sports.) When my client didn't fulfill his father's dreams, his father brutally punished him by withdrawing his love. At family gatherings, his father shamed and shunned him. Terminally ill with cancer, my client's father eventually made amends on his deathbed. The reconciliation helped, but by then much emotional damage had been done.

Perhaps your family likes or praises you for being an emotional or physical caretaker of them. Or, if society has viewed you as "less than" because of your skin color or gender or orientation, you may have deeply internalized the oppression. Others in your social group may criticize you if you see yourself differently or try to "rise above your class."

People in recovery sometimes experience resistance when they change for the better. The family homeostasis is disrupted. Family members think, *I liked you better when you were drinking; you were funny and now you're uptight.* Or, family members got an ego boost from feeling superior to the addict. Family members may be reluctant to look at their own part in the difficulties and resist change.

More challenging still are the obstacles of an internal nature

—when our mind is convinced that the stories of our deficiency are *true*.

Leaving the World of Mental Construction

Where and how do we begin our escape, releasing our inner critics with their script and stage set? We start with the fundamentals of mindfulness. Here we will not try to rid ourselves of our gang of inner critics, banishing them to deeper realms of repression and therefore rendering them more dangerous still. "*No, no, dear one,*" as one of my mentors used to say. Instead, the mindfulness approach befriends our inner critics first, recognizing them, and loosening our identification with their stories of shame and inadequacy.

Here we turn to our next mindfulness slogan, *Rest in the openness of mind,* to guide the way. We begin by holding more spaciousness in our minds: more room around our stories; less conviction that our mental formations are the truth; less holding on to the critical narratives about ourselves. Hence, we take up meditating and resting in openness of mind. We realize through mindfulness that our stories are essentially empty, moving, and fluctuating interpretations. We open to the reality of the myriad causes and conditions that influence our reactions, other people's actions, and our interpretations of them both. Think back to our two airline pilots. Which view was correct?

A well-known Zen teaching story likens our minds to living in a house with the windows closed and doors locked while outside there is fresh sky and shining sun. Why would a person want to live like this? Yet we do, many times because we don't see what we are doing. Our thoughts seem real. The inner critics are familiar companions.

Rest in the openness of mind instructs us to loosen up and open up. We realize our stories may not be true—maybe, just maybe, not *entirely* true. We cultivate openness of mind by learning to observe the mind rather than believe the stories of the mind, build awareness of the body, and stay with our feelings long enough to explore them.

> *Rest in the openness of mind.*
> *Openness of mind . . .*
> *Opening the mind . . .*

The Four Levels of Mindfulness Training

In mindfulness, we are taught to practice awareness in a progression of areas, one building upon the other. Each area will help you discover openness of mind.

Awareness of the Body

The ancient language of a teaching text refers to "awareness of the body *in* the body." Notice when we are breathing in that we *are* breathing in. Notice as we are breathing out that we *are* breathing out. Learn to feel our legs as we walk, hear the sounds of the birds in the sky, notice the verdant greens of the grass after a fresh rain, and experience the taste of our food as we eat.

With the classic body scan practice taught in mindfulness-based stress reduction,[5] we become intimate with the sensations of our body. We notice which areas of the body hold stress and tension and stay present to the here-and-now flow of sensation. Body awareness helps us know that we have a tight neck or stomach now rather than hours or days later when we wake up and say, *Wow! Am I stiff. I have a pain in my shoulder.* We train so we can be *in* our body, aware of what is happening when it is happening.

Awareness of Emotions

Once we become mindful of the body, we next train in "awareness of the feelings in the feelings." Here we are breathing and noting the emotions as they arise in us—the deeper feeling that a tight neck or tight shoulder is holding: *Oh! This is anger!* Or, the hairs rising on the back of the neck are fear; the burning sensation in the chest is shame. Awareness of the feelings in the feelings is not as easy as it sounds (that is, if it even sounds easy).

My husband, Jim, and I met up with our dear friends Maddie and Lucas at a restaurant in Minneapolis for Indian food. The samosas and shrimp biryani were spicy and perfectly prepared, making for a wonderful meal. Still, the ambient noise in the crowded restaurant made it difficult to talk. After dinner we opted to have our coffees at another location, hoping to visit without shouting.

We consulted Siri on our iPhones to locate the nearest coffeehouse and both cars followed her directions. The first espresso bar we checked had already closed for the evening. No parking at the next one. All tables were full at the third one. Five stops later, we scored a coffee bar that was open, had parking, and seats available on a Friday night. Hooray!

During the drive I turned from impatient to annoyed to entirely crabby: "What's the matter with these places? Why don't they have parking available? How come this place is showing up on the Maps app when it's already closed? This was a *dumb* idea to go out for coffee."

I kept jabbering until my husband said, "What's going on? Why are you getting so uptight?" I had noticed my irritability but not the "what's going on?" part. Jim's question caused me to pause and look inward. I realized I was actually feeling sadness. My dear friend Maddie is having more and more memory loss, and I wonder if it isn't early Alzheimer's. Without quite realizing it, I had been stepping in throughout dinner to help her. Her eyes seemed blank, not entirely "there." Maddie has been one of my dearest friends for more than forty years and what I really felt was grief. Losing the "old Maddie" evoked sorrow that was at first cloaked in crabby. It's typical of me—get angry first, then (hopefully) realize what feeling is underneath.

This, then, is the second level of awareness training, feeling the feelings *in* the feelings. Try to notice the sorrow straight away or at least recognize that irritability might be a cover for grief arising. With repeated practice, mindfulness helps us get closer to the emotion in the moment it arises. And don't be discouraged by the word *repeated*. Research suggests that increased practice translates into increased effects.

Awareness of Thoughts

The next level of mindfulness is noticing the "thoughts *in* the thoughts." Here we start to notice how often the mind is interpreting—writing a script, building a story to explain what we experience.

Gabby and Doug had been in couples counseling throughout the summer to reconcile after a year's separation. Gentle sunlight spilling through the blinds couldn't ease the tension in my clinical office. They sat on the edge of the rust-corduroy sofa, rigid and tight. Both stared straight ahead, talking to me instead of to each other, reporting on a conflict from the previous weekend.

"I felt restless—lonely, I think—and wanted to connect last Saturday afternoon," Gabby said. "So I asked Doug what he was reading. He didn't look up or even bother to answer, buried behind his book. Like usual! It made me really mad that he doesn't make much effort to connect. *He just doesn't care.* You're damn right I started yelling at him. I had to do something to get his attention."

Doug crossed his arms around his chest. "She is *so* unreasonable. I was reading, for crap's sake. Is that a crime? Gabby has anger problems and she won't admit it. No matter what I do, it's never good enough. Whenever I try to please her, she just raises the bar. *I can't win.*"

When I pointed out that they both were interpreting the meaning of what each other did based on their history and its emotional baggage, Doug said with disgust, "No. This is *not* my 'interpretation.' IT'S THE WAY . . . IT . . . WAS."

Doug was entirely convinced he was right—that his view was objective and true. But he wasn't. He wasn't aware that he was interpreting through his portable stage set, a subjective inner narrative that only had some to do with Gabby. He didn't have the advantage of practicing mindfulness, despite having been treated for depression a number of years earlier.

We cannot be right in thinking that our inner critics are right. The venerable Vietnamese meditation master Thích Nhất Hạnh says it like this: "Attachment to views is the greatest impediment to the spiritual path. Bound to narrow views, one becomes so entangled that it is no longer possible to let the door of truth open."[6]

In mindfulness meditation, we spend time noticing our thoughts, watching them with an observing self and putting mental space around our stories so we can see them in action. The trick is to notice the story in the midst of it—or, second best, soon thereafter.

> *Rest in the openness of mind . . .*
> *Open the mind . . .*
> *Observe the mind . . .*

Awareness of the Objects of the Mind

This is the most advanced level of mindfulness training. Here we become aware of the deeper beliefs that feed our stories, especially the ones that fuel our inner critics, such as:

- I must have done something wrong for her or him to treat me like this.

- I don't deserve to have love.
- I am fundamentally not good enough.

These are the objects, or *internal formations,* of the mind. The sticklers. These are the thought patterns and stubborn viewpoints or pathogenic beliefs that hurt us, the lifeblood of our inner critics. These are the beliefs that cause dis-ease such as shame, defined by psychotherapists Ronald and Patricia Potter-Efron as "the painful belief that we are deficient."[7]

The term *internal formation* as used in Buddhist psychology conjures a powerful image for me. *Formation* suggests a stalagmite or stalactite created by the drip, drip, drip of water over time. Likewise, an internal formation is created by an idea about ourselves that we learned while growing up, implicitly or explicitly, and absorbed unconsciously in slow accretions over time.

Examples of internal formations include our culturally conditioned images and beliefs about *man, woman, black, white, gay,* or *straight.* Each time we think such thoughts and believe those ideas we etch their neuropathway in our brains more deeply. Our thoughts repeated time and again are like the drips of water that make the belief more and more solid, more and more real. Without even realizing, we believe ourselves and become convinced our internal formation is true.

When our minds are filled by internal formations with admonishments of our inner critics, their voice becomes our universe. If my inner voice says, *You're too fat,* I believe her even if I'm at a healthy weight. The problem is that we believe our stories.

Some people object to this: *What do you mean, it's just an idea I have about myself?* I invite them to consider the paradigms of history—when we *knew,* for example, that the Earth was flat, that we were the center of the universe, and that a manmade heavier-than-air piece of machinery could not take flight. Internal formations arise like those paradigms and wield corresponding power.

The idea of resting in the openness of mind is to free ourselves from the activity of our "nuisance mind," that busy, monkey-mind that is filled with stories and criticisms of ourselves and others. This is not like the work of other therapies where we try to make the mind be still or to replace the stories of our inner critics with new, more rational, positive thoughts. Instead, mind-training changes our *relationship* with those thoughts. We learn to dis-identify with their noise. Here we rest the mind in meditative openness and simplicity and space.

Mindfulness Meditation Is More Like "Not Meditating" Than Meditating

People tend to think that meditation is *making* the mind be quiet and getting rid of discursive thought—*doing* something. Instead, with mindfulness, we relax with whatever thoughts and feelings come up and—this is the tricky part—just let our thoughts and sensations go on by, neither pushing away our inner critics nor grabbing on to their stories.

My husband and I spent a few months in Mexico last winter to get away from the frigid cold and deep-freeze temperatures of

January and February in Minnesota. At a social gathering, we were introduced to a friend of a friend with the opening, "You both share an interest in meditation." Louise started studying mindfulness meditation some years ago, at the suggestion of her physician. He said it would likely help her with the stress of her power job.

"For the first several years, I didn't think I was very good at meditation and it was super frustrating!" Louise said. "I just could *not* get my mind to settle. I kept trying and failing at getting my thoughts to quiet down. My monkey-mind is impossible!"

Louise went on to say that she was now taking a class with a new teacher. "Right off, he told me not to try so hard. [He said,] 'Don't try to be "good" at meditating. Just let your mind rest and relax with whatever comes up. Notice your thoughts without judging yourself, and when you get distracted, don't worry. Just bring yourself back to your breath and begin again (and again and again).'" She said this new approach was a breakthrough, and asked, "Is that how you do meditation?"

With a slight nod, I said, "That is what meditation *is*."

I felt sad that Louise had taken classes for years and, in that time, hadn't learned the fundamental practice of resting in the openness of mind. (It's important to have an experienced teacher with good training. More on that later.) Paradoxically, not trying so hard to meditate is a better way to meditate.

I received this suggestion years ago at Mount Madonna Center, which stretches across acres of mountaintop redwood forest and grassland overlooking Monterey Bay in Northern California. Lush, pacific grounds are interposed there with birdsong and the ringing of temple bells. My husband and I had come for a weekend retreat with Tenshin Reb Anderson, one of our beloved teachers from the San Francisco Zen Center.

The conference room at the center was beige on beige with a solo candle holding vigil for the small wooden statue of the Buddha. Between the fifty-some participants, the hours of sitting meditation, and the late afternoon sunlight, the space had become sticky and close. Tenshin-roshi's voice was also hoarse from a head cold, almost a whisper. After his lecture on being in the present moment and "resting in suchness,"[8] he rasped, "What are your questions?"

A young, petite woman ventured this: "Tenshin, I notice that I have been struggling with sleepiness during your talk, finding it hard to keep my eyes open. And, I realize that I'm *often* tired at this time of day. I'm so good at being responsible, going to my job every day and raising my son. I practice hard at meditation, too." Tearing up, she continued, "I simply have no idea how to stop 'doing.' *I don't know how to rest.* Can you help me with this?"

Tenshin-roshi looked at her with immense kindness and said, "Resting is good. And, you should be very kind to yourself about your struggle."

My husband gently poked me and said, "You, too."

We are not trying to make ourselves *be* a certain way when we meditate. In fact, the venerable Yongey Mingyur Rinpoche,[9] whose name means "precious jewel," introduces meditation with the following "non-meditating exercise" that his grand-father taught his father, and his father taught him. All were Tibetan monks and honored meditation teachers.

> *Rest in the openness of mind . . .*
> *Rest the mind . . .*
> *Just rest. . . .*

Non-Meditating Exercise—Resting the Mind

Don't try to make yourself do anything except sit down on the cushion or in your chair, hold the posture, and breathe. Once seated, simply be present to and curious about whatever arises. Observe your mind as if watching clouds pass in the sky. Acknowledge, with kindness, whatever is happening. The idea in this practice is to simply rest the mind for three minutes.

Try This:

- **Sit with your spine straight.** Make sure you can breathe easily, with the body relaxed.

- **Allow your mind to rest.** Let it go anywhere it goes. Whatever happens—or doesn't happen—is part of the mental experiment. Simply notice it. You might feel physically comfortable or uncomfortable. You might hear sounds or smell smells in your environment. You might get lost in thoughts or become aware of feelings of anger, sadness, fear, or other emotions. Just go with any of it. Anything that happens—or doesn't happen—is simply part of the experience.

> • **When the three minutes are up, reflect.** Ask yourself: How was this experiment? Don't judge or evaluate, or try to explain. Just review what happened and how you felt.

Rest . . .
Allow yourself to rest . . .
Hold an open, nonjudging mind . . .

Rest . . . in the openness . . . of mind.
Rest . . . in openness . . .
Rest.

Learn to let down.
Learn to slow down.
Maybe for one of the first times . . .
*   we can slow down . . .*

Resting in the Openness of Big Mind

Years ago, over tomato and avocado sandwiches, a friend told me about his time in the contemplative monastery called Nada Hermitage in Sedona, Arizona. He described the beauty of living a simple life of silence, meditation, and manual work. His story inspired my own sojourn to the red rock lands of the ancient Hopi people. Free of any real obligations and with enough money in my pocket for a tank of gas, I was compelled to go.

At that time, Nada was located on a wide expanse of high desert where coyotes howled at the moon in the night. The community, which consisted of crudely built one-room hermitages, was an experiment in Christian–Zen fusion started by a Carmelite priest. Think Thomas Merton meets the Dalai Lama meets the radical influences of the post–Vatican II era of the 1970s.

It was here that I first learned about rest. I was wound tight, my brain's hyperactive amygdala on alert for danger—leftover vigilance from my childhood of violence and alcoholism. I valued order and control. My body held the fear and the grief of those early experiences and I didn't want my soft spots exposed, thank you. I had been super-responsible since the age of seven when I was the kid calling the police for help while my mother was getting hit by my alcoholic father.

Nada cradled me in its arms. It was as if the ancient peoples had left their mark in the earth itself because Nada emanated peace. One of the practices we did there, somewhat archaic, was a twenty-four-hour vigil during the full moon each month. A member of the monastic community was "on duty" each hour of the day and night, holding wake in the chapel. I usually chose between two and three o'clock in the morning.

A flashlight wasn't necessary in the cloudless Arizona night with red dirt paths illumined by eerie, brilliant moonlight. In the wee hours of the morning, I'd make my way from my hermitage to the chapel, dug into the earth like a kiva (a chamber built into the ground by Pueblo Indians for religious rites). I went down the steps into the sacred room filled with the smells of sage incense and candle wax. The quietude was palpable. I was alone but for a single holy icon, candlelight flickering shadows on the limestone walls.

There was nothing else to do, nowhere else to go. Breathing in and out, resting the mind. No judgment, no threat, the quiet more powerful than the chorus of inner critics. This was one of my first moments of rest, a slight unwinding in the body, a slight opening of the mind to just observe, swaddled in the velvet silence. *Ahhhhhh.*

A friend sent me this poem, *Free and Easy,* by Lama Gendun Rinpoche. The words resonate to my experience.

> *Happiness cannot be found*
> *through great effort and willpower*
> *but is already present, in open relaxation*
> *and letting go.*
>
> *Rest . . .*
> *Rest . . . in the openness . . .*
> *Rest . . . in the openness . . . of mind.*

As one learned meditation teacher says, "The idea [of this slogan] is that there is a resting place of some kind. . . . You have some kind of relaxation with yourself. . . . You don't have to run away from yourself all the time in order to get something outside. You can just come home and relax. The idea is to return to home-sweet-home."[10]

Once we have meditated with this slogan, the contrast between the insanity engendered by our inner critics and the freedom of openness of mind becomes clear. We aren't as easily fooled that the narrative of our minds is true. Our personal *Truman Show* cracks open.

We build upon this fundamental meditation practice as we consider each of our remaining *lojong* phrases, coming home to resting the mind whenever we wander. Nudging ourselves back with kindness.

> . . . *Rest in the openness . . . of mind.*

Stay Close (and Do Nothing)

Once we have created space around our thought patterns with the slogan *Rest in the openness of mind,* we are able to see our inner critics for what they are: harsh, learned, and often delusionary ideas about ourselves and others.

Our next mindfulness slogan—*Stay close (and do nothing)*—instructs us to make a simple but profound shift in how we relate to our inner critics. Instead of seeking to change our thoughts, mindfulness advises us to change our *relationship* with our thoughts. Instead of pushing away our inner critics, we investigate them. I mentioned this idea in chapter 2. Now we'll explore it in detail.

When Not to Stay Close to Your Inner Critics

As you begin this chapter, remember that mind-training is most effective when balanced with self-compassion and loving-kindness toward ourselves. This is especially true with the slogan explored in this chapter.

In fact, there are signs to indicate that working with this slogan—and possibly doing any mindfulness meditation—might not be appropriate for you right now. These signs include:

- Hearing voices in your head that seem real—even when those voices try to tell you things that are highly questionable or simply untrue.

- Feeling overwhelmed or flooded by painful thoughts and emotions.

- The tendency to *disassociate,* sometimes described as "spacing out," "checking out," "getting lost in my own world," "disconnecting," or "leaving your body."

Any of the above can be an issue for people in early recovery, or for those with a history of child abuse or other trauma. If you have any such experiences, please consult with a psychotherapist *before* continuing with mind-training or any other meditation practices. These practices are helpful only for people who already have adequate coping skills in place.

Become Intimate with What Is Unwelcome in You

If you're anything like me, you've wanted to get rid of your inner critics. Banish them. Cut them out and remove them. Make them stop haunting the mind. Shut them up.

During my addiction days, I used amphetamines to escape from the berating of my inner critics, attempting to anesthetize their voices. And, I really wanted meditation practice to be the great tranquilizer medicine to get those inner critics the hell out of here.

Surprise (at least it was for me)! That isn't how meditation works. If we try to get rid of the unwanted parts of ourselves, they are more likely to come back in the form of symptoms such as headaches, ulcers, obsessiveness, depression, or anxiety. The way of mindfulness suggests that we stop running away and instead *turn toward* what is unwelcome in us—a radical and scary idea.

An old Zen story points to the idea of getting to know our inner mind as the path to liberation. A meditation master had an attendant assigned to help him. Among the attendant's many jobs, one was to carry the robe for the senior teacher. In this case, the forty-second ancestor, Ryozan Enkan,[1] was carrying the robe for the forty-first ancestor, Dōan Kanshi.[2]

They paused on their walk because the teacher needed to put his robe on. Kanshi said to his disciple: "What is the business under the patched robe?" ("Under the patched robe" is a metaphor for meditation practice; monks made their robes from scraps of cloth stitched together, as had Gautama Buddha, in the spirit of renunciation of worldliness.)

Enkan had no answer. So he in turn asked his teacher, "What is the business under the patched robe?"

Kanshi said, "Intimacy. Intimacy."

Upon hearing his teacher's answer, Enkan became enlightened. He bowed to Kanshi in great gratitude, and tears were flowing.

Kanshi asked, "What have you understood? Can you express it?"

Enkan said, "What happens in meditation practice? Intimacy."

Kanshi said, "Intimacy and even greater intimacy."[3]

This Zen tale suggests that meditation practice establishes a deep familiarity with ourselves and, therefore, with others and life itself. This includes staying close with our inner critics—the antithesis of what we want to do.

Emotional awareness and intimacy with our inner critics, as uncomfortable as it may be, is an opportunity to awaken greater compassion for ourselves and others, offering a great value to our spiritual life. The venerable Norman Fischer, Zen priest and founder of the *Every Day Zen* organization, says that the investigation of afflictive emotions (including our inner critics) "is the most beneficial of all practices."[4]

Hence, the slogan *Stay close (and do nothing)*. The traditional translation is actually *Stay close to what provokes you*. For our discussion, I invite you to think about our inner critics as the provoking entity. This slogan invites us to stay close to our inner critics, explore them, and *become intimate* as a way to begin releasing them. Sometimes you have to "go in" before you can "get out" of the tangle. Just for now, we are invited to sit in meditation and do nothing but befriend our inner critics. Mindfulness practice teaches this fundamental turnabout: Instead of banishing the unwanted parts of ourselves, explore them with curiosity, interest, and nonjudgment.

We develop awareness when we sit in meditation, rest the mind, and notice the fixed views that we hold. Many of us don't recognize our inner critics because their voice is so familiar; it sounds like reality. And the moment you observe the mind in action, the thinking brain (neocortex) becomes engaged. In response, we *observe* rather than *believe* our thoughts. With the help of our gray matter, we are less likely to believe the inner critic's story. The ability to develop an observing mind to *see* rather than *believe* is essential to change. When we see our stories, we can dis-identify with them.

Once back home after my months at Nada, I began to work with a spiritual director at the Cenacle Retreat House in Wayzata, Minnesota. Sister Mary Sharon Riley, R.C., stood tall with an erect posture that conjured memories of the Catholic nuns at my high school, the Academy of the Holy Angels, where I was made to walk with phone books balanced on my head. Mary Sharon was another Irish force to be reckoned with: bright, articulate, strong, and fierce in her caring for me.

We talked about my inner critics and how they interfered with having a loving image or experience of a Higher Power. Mary Sharon said that meditation and prayer develop discernment—the ability to notice inner critics. She said it was not unlike recognizing "the smell of a rotten egg in your refrigerator." We notice the smell rather than eat the poisonous food. In Twelve Step recovery, we have a similar expression that describes a negative mind-set as "stinking thinking." These are the kinds of thoughts that lead to relapse and self-destructive acts. I had never thought about my harsh inner narrative as being like stinky eggs in my refrigerator before. I can almost smell them now, and it's a rancid odor.

Stay close . . .

Stay . . .

Stay . . . stay . . . just stay . . .

Learn to Stay with Your Inner Experience

The venerable Pema Chödrön, an ordained nun (acharya[5] in the Shambhala Buddhist lineage), is one of the foremost teachers of *lojong* practice in the West. She talks about meditation as a process of "learning to stay" with our emotions and becoming intimate with our inner self. She compares this to training a puppy. If we discipline a young puppy by yelling at it, beating it, or being cruel, we will likely end up with an obedient but cowering animal. He might follow our commands to *sit, heel,* or *fetch,* but he will also be nervous and confused. Or, he will become aggressive and chew at the sofa when unattended. Kindness works better when training an animal; veterinarians recommend it because it is effective and humane.[6]

People-creatures, too, need kindness in order to be flexible and confident when challenging situations arrive at their door. When our mind wanders in meditation, we work with it similar to how we train a puppy. We firmly but kindly nudge ourselves to stay with our inner experience. We encourage ourselves to *Stay close (and do nothing),* learning to be with ourselves just as we are.

Again, meditation is not about spiritually bypassing our life experiences and achieving a state of permanent bliss. Many people think this, as if meditation offers another drug-like escape from the difficulties of reality. Rather, we sit in meditation and stay present to ourselves under all kinds of conditions and through all kinds of moods. Can you imagine *listening* to your inner critics instead of scolding them into submission or trying to shoo them away?

"Stay close" is the first step of deeper self-compassion. This practice is simple in that during meditation we are often calling ourselves back from distractions of a mundane nature: *What should I eat for breakfast? . . . That car that just went by outside needs a new muffler. . . . I wonder how much money I have left in my checkbook this month?* Yet the point of meditation is *not* to silence the monkey-mind. The point is to change our relationship with our monkey-minds, to keep coming back, to notice and let go of our thoughts—to *stay*.

> *Stay close . . .*
> *Stay close to what provokes you . . .*
> *Stay close to your inner critics . . .*

The following was inspired by a piece by Pema Chödrön.

> *Are you agitated? Stay!*
> *Find yourself nursing a list of resentments? Stay!*
> *Are you bored with meditation? Stay!*
> *Sore back and aching knees? Stay!*
> *Wondering what's for dinner? Stay!*
> *Wrapping yourself in grief or self-pity? Stay!*
> *Checking the clock? Stay!*

Breathing and Noting Meditation Practice

The fundamental practice of mindfulness meditation is called breathing and noting. We concentrate on the sensations of breath in the body, notice our thoughts as if we were a still mountain watching the clouds pass by in the sky.

Noting is a silent acknowledgment of what happens in the mind. It cultivates honesty, nonjudgment, awareness, and an ongoing sense of the present moment. Here's how to practice it.

- *Breathe naturally.* Gently bring awareness to the breath, keeping the attention at one precise point, such as the nostrils or the belly. When breathing in, note *in;* when breathing out, note *out.*

- *Greet distractions with kindness and curiosity.* As soon as you become aware that you have wandered, use bare attention to notice the nature of the distraction. Silently tag the distraction as, for example, "thinking" or "feeling" or "pain" or "resistance."

- *As the process of noting becomes refined and subtler, note specific qualities of the distraction.* For example, instead of noting "thinking," you might notice "planning" or "daydreaming" or "worrying" or "shaming." Gently bring your awareness back to the breath and begin again to notice breathing *in,* breathing *out.*

The Origins of Inner Critics

Until you understand how your inner critics began, you'll have trouble releasing them. Rather than attempting to exorcise them, turn toward them with curiosity and interest to ask, "Where did my inner critics get these ideas? How did they take root in me and why are they so strong?"[7]

After becoming aware of the "stinky eggs" in my psyche through meditation practice, I began to realize that many of my inner critics were born of learned ideas and empty of true substance. Catholic theologian Thomas Keating says, "The stories of our inner critics are (primarily) overlays on top of [our] true self, obscuring our conscious contact with it. Meditation is a practice that opens up conscious contact with our True Self. It suggests that much of what we have learned about ourselves is wrong."[8]

Inner critics develop from messages we received while growing up that are now deeply internalized (*introjected*) into beliefs we carry about ourselves. We carry the ideas, emotions, and sensations from earlier formative life experiences—from our parents, teachers, coaches, churches, and society—even though our situation may have changed. (As I write this, an image of five-foot-zero-inch Sister Marcella, the scourge of my third-grade class, comes to mind. I can still recall the edge in her voice and the belittling sound of her sarcasm. I suppose because it was so much like my dá's manner at home.)

According to recent work by Greg Hajcak Proudfit, a clinical psychologist at Stony Brook University, critical parenting trains a child's brain to overly emphasize mistakes. When we make a mistake, the medial prefrontal cortex—just behind the center of the forehead—produces an electrical pattern called *error-related negativity*, or ERN. This pattern is the brain's way of helping us keep from making similar mistakes in the future. Research suggests that genetics can account for variations in the strength of the ERN among individuals. Proudfit's work suggests that exposure to harsh criticism also comes into play. According to Proudfit, children who are exposed to harsh criticism learn to internalize parental feedback until the ERN, normally a caution sign, becomes a trigger for anxiety. This causes children to overreact to their mistakes.[9] If we don't recognize an overactive ERN and its critical story, we can't release it. We have no hope of building a *loving* superego that guides us through life. If we stay close, we can transform.

> *And so . . .*
> *Stay close . . .*
> *Stay close to what provokes you . . .*

Ask Your Inner Critics in for Tea

Although we may want to purge our inner critics, both Eastern mindfulness teachings and certain Western psychologies suggest that we first seek to understand them. This model of inner healing invites us to hang out with and befriend our inner critics, seeking to appreciate their function at a deeper level.

Stay close could even be seen as inviting our inner critics in for tea and a visit as if they were old friends. According to the venerable meditation teacher Thích Nhất Hạnh this metaphor of "welcoming our unwanted parts" begins with a story from the life of the historical Guatama Buddha.[10]

Buddha was hanging out with his disciples, living in a cold cave in northern India along with his handsome cousin, Ananda. Many guests came, and they always wanted to have a cup of tea with the Buddha. The Buddha could not just receive guests all day, so Ananda tried to help, assigning himself the job of protecting the Buddha from too many visitors.

One morning while Ananda was doing walking meditation outside Buddha's cave, he saw someone coming in his direction. He had the impression that he knew this person but just forgot his name. When that person neared, he recognized him as Mara—in Eastern lore, the figure that personifies evil. Mara's face was veiled and he was always trying to tempt the Buddha with power, money, or beautiful women.

When Ananda realized Mara was approaching, he said, "What are you doing here?"

"I want to visit the Buddha," Mara said. "I want to see him."

"Why should you want to see the Buddha?" Ananda replied. "I don't think the Buddha has time for you. Actually, I don't think that he will see you at all. You are the *enemy* of the Buddha."

When Ananda went in to announce the visit of Mara, he hoped that the Buddha would decline. But to Ananda's surprise, the Buddha smiled beautifully and said, "Mara, wonderful! Ask him to come in . . . Ananda, please make us tea."

Ananda was not happy. The idea of making tea for Mara was not pleasant. But since the Buddha had asked, Ananda went into a corner and began to make tea.

When the tea was offered to the Buddha and the guest, Ananda stood behind the Buddha and tried to be mindful of what the Buddha would need. But it did not seem that the Buddha needed anything. He just looked at Mara in a very loving way and said, "Dear friend, how have you been? Is everything okay?"

This teaching parable illustrates the mindfulness approach to working with our inner critics. An interesting aspect is how Mara is depicted as a veiled figure to represent our delusions, things we don't want to deal with or see, as "the enemy." Here the Buddha teaches us how to approach our enemies within and without, understand them, and befriend them. Rather than run away, keeping ourselves veiled in delusion and denial, we invite our inner critics in for tea. We have a chat. We welcome each of them like an old friend.

This was Jennie's experience. She was never angry—depressed, but never angry. She was also forty pounds overweight. She cut herself and had difficulty maintaining an intimate relationship. But she was, without fail, pleasant to others: the quintessential "Minnesota nice." Her inner critic, on the other hand, was vicious.

In a session one day, I guided her in a meditation on "welcoming her anger as an old friend." Jennie saw her anger in the image of a Tasmanian devil—stocky build, black fur, pungent odor, with an extremely loud and disturbing screech. "He was speaking gibberish and didn't make any sense," she said.

This was precisely the attitude that made Jennie repress her angry feelings. Her family viewed anger toward each other as unreasonable and not making any sense. Rather than buck the family system—and be looked at as a Tasmanian devil in her family—Jennie redirected her frustrations against herself. Blaming herself protected her from feeling grief about her family's limitations and their inability to be emotionally honest.

Welcoming Your Inner Critic Like an Old Friend

In mind-training, we get to know our critics and accept them as part of us. We allow them in, touch them, let them go. We don't have to resist them. This is the wisdom of the practice.

I learned the following meditation from the venerable Thích Nhất Hạnh, founder of Plum Village in France. It instructs us to welcome our inner critics—invite them in, ask them to pull up a chair, visit for a while, and have some tea as we would with an old friend.

Try This:

- Begin with five minutes of mindful breathing.

- Take the next few moments to recognize each feeling as it arises. For example, look at your guilt and recognize it as guilt. This is the practice of "feeling the feelings in the feelings."

- Let the feeling be. In the words of Thích Nhất Hạnh, "It is best not to say, 'Go away, Fear. I don't like you. You are not me.' It is much more effective to say, 'Hello, Fear. How are you today?' Doing this may not be easy at first, but remember that you are more than just your feelings. As long as mindfulness is present, you will not drown in your feeling. In fact, you begin transforming it in the very moment you give birth to awareness in yourself."[11]

- Take the next five to ten minutes to visit with your emotions: anxiety, anger, self-pity, fear, worry, boredom, shame, or whatever feeling arises. Ask them to pull up a chair and stay a while.

- Linger here with your imagination for a few moments. Picture the inner critic in your mind's eye:

  - What is its face?

  - How is it dressed?

  - Where in your house does it come to sit?

  - What does it have to say?

  - How is this part—this inner critic—trying to protect you, even if it's in a maladaptive or distorted way? What has its job been in your life?

  - What would you like to ask it?

  - How do you feel about having it as your guest?

- Notice what you learn about this inner critic. Turn your concentration to accepting it, warmly and graciously, despite its muddy feet, rude manners, or threatening face: *Oh, I know you. You are familiar, an old friend. How are you today?*

- Now, complete the meditation with five minutes of breathing, calming, and letting go. You can do this by saying to yourself, "Breathing in, I calm myself. Breathing out, I smile." Then, "in, calm" with the in-breath and "out, smile" with the out-breath.

Take a few moments to jot down your emerging thoughts and images from this meditation in a personal journal. If you repeat this practice over time, it reduces the size and ugliness of your distressing emotions.

How Inner Critics Seek to Protect Us—
Even When They Harm Us

The restaurant our friends chose for dinner was at the end of a curving frontage road. A blackboard listing four daily specials hung just inside the entry. My husband scanned the many gray-haired patrons and said, "We fit right in here." Our friends frequent this restaurant because the specials are good—full entrée, choice of potato, and vegetable of the day, all for $12.00. And, it comes with a side of mixed green salad.

Lew chuckled, "Old people like to come here but all they ever order are the daily specials. I'm glad you guys are here, though, because Maxine is having a bad day. Maybe you can cheer her up."

"Oh no," I said. "What's wrong, Maxine?"

"I got a haircut yesterday and I hate my bangs. They are *too short*."

I know from our forty-some years of friendship that Maxine has a thing about her hair. When it's not right, it really bothers her. Hair is a trigger for lots of us, a symbol of attractiveness and charm for many women. Over the years, however, I've discovered that a bad haircut actually grows out.

When a haircut triggers Maxine, she goes down the rabbit hole. Her inner critic starts by telling her she looks stupid, and then moves on to all sorts of other things that are wrong with her. This particular evening she said she wanted to hide her face under a hat or not go out of the house. She said her mood went from embarrassment about her bangs to thinking that:

> *She had nothing decent to wear*
> *to go to dinner tonight . . .*
>
> *To deciding she should go shopping*
> *for better clothes . . .*
>
> *To believing she had no time to go*
> *shopping for clothes . . .*
>
> *Because she wasn't a very organized person*
> *and had bad taste anyway . . .*
>
> *So why bother?*

"But, help me understand," I asked, "Why does it upset you so very much?" I knew my dear friend had been bullied terribly in school when she was young, and it dawned on me for some reason to ask about this. "Did you by chance get bullied about your hair when you were in school?"

Maxine thought for a moment. Then she began to talk about her terrible experiences in country school. She started first grade at the age of five because her mother was ill. Maxine needed to be away at school so her mother could recuperate. She was in a one-room school with kids from kindergarten to eighth grade, and the older boys ruled the playground.

"Those mean eighth graders threw me in a hole under the bridge and taunted me. I was afraid I was going to drown and when I tried to get out, they pushed me back down. Finally, the bell rang and we all had to go back into the classroom and I escaped."

"Were they making fun of your hair when they started to bully you?"

"As a matter of fact, I think so. My aunt was a beautician and gave me a haircut the night before. She cut my bangs too short and they looked really stupid. The boys were making fun of my hair when they held me down. I never really thought about those two things being connected until now. Maybe that's why I always hate my hair so much."

Jim and I and Lew offered sympathy. "Sounds like school was terrible for you when you were little."

"Yes, I hated that country school! Absolutely hated it. Still hate that school, in fact."

Recent social research says that the impact of bullying in school can be worse than emotional or physical abuse at home. My friend Maxine was carrying remnants of the emotional imprint more than fifty years later.

Maxine discovered how inner critics jump in when we are about to feel emotions we are not comfortable with or think we can't handle. Our critics try to protect us from suppressed pain from the past, a traumatic experience, or feelings we don't want to feel. They direct our attention away from a memory or emotion—such as grief or hurt or anger—to criticism of ourselves or others instead. If we can understand an inner critic's "job," we can show it compassion rather than fight it. This in turn helps the inner critic let go of its judgments.

It may not seem like an inner critic that says, *Hey, fat boy* or *What have you got between those ears, sawdust?* is trying to help. But it might be. A harsh, critical voice can serve to preempt criticism from others or try to keep you from failing in the eyes of your peers. If you pause to reflect on formative experiences, buried memories, and messages you received in childhood, you can uncover the job your inner critics hold. As psychotherapist Richard Schwartz says, "Once I let go of the need to change [an inner critic], and just become curious, it could let down its guard and reveal its predicament."[12] Then real change begins to happen.

This turnaround from trying to rid ourselves of our inner critics to seeking to understand them is both fascinating and different from our usual strategy. Instead of immediately trying to exorcise an inner critic, we first look into how the voice developed, where it came from, and how it may be trying to help. We stay close and for the moment do nothing but listen and investigate without judgment.

Staying close is a difficult, challenging, liberating process. Yet an old body of wisdom tells us to just stay close to ourselves, even if it's for just one more breath than we think we can stand. This stance itself waters the seeds of kindness within us, growing conscious contact with our True Self. In breathing and noting meditation, for example, we call our monkey-mind back to the present moment using kindness. Each time we do this, we "mess with" our inner critics. We come back to the sensations of the breath, let go of judgment, and begin again in the next moment. As we investigate rather than expel the unwanted parts of ourselves and others, we build a kinder voice.

Stay close . . .

Stay close to our brokenness . . .

Stay close to what provokes you . . .

Reflect on Messages from How You Grew Up

If you are like many of us, you may have tried to forget about painful experiences, burying them deep in your mind. In that case, some of your inner critics may activate when you get close to the emotional hurt, "protecting" your wounded inner child from remembering and working through the trauma or pain.

Think of a time you were humiliated, grief stricken, terrified, or abandoned. What have you tried to do with the memories, sensations, and emotions that came from those events?

Try This:

- Reflect on what it was like to grow up in your family.[13] What do you remember about getting criticized by your parents or other significant caretakers? Did this criticism arise for a particular personality trait or behavior such as being too loud, too timid, too noisy, too nosy, or too lazy?

- How did family members let you know they disapproved?

- How did your family typically react to anger, to sadness, to fear, to taking risks?

- Was your family concerned or unconcerned with what the neighbors would say? What other members of the extended family thought? How much did you feel a need to live up to a certain image for them?

- How did you feel when you disappointed or angered one of your parents or caregivers?

- When you recall your friends in high school, how did they separate the "ins" from the "outs"? How did they treat people who were "different"?

Naming Your Inner Critics Weakens Them

One way to stay close is to give each member of the gang of inner critics a name. In the mindful practice of breathing and noting, we lessen the power of an inner critic at the moment we observe rather than believe its story. Now we further lessen its power by looking at it with enough compassion to greet it. After we christen our critic, we can then ask, *How was or is this critic trying to "help"?*

Stay close . . .
Stay close to your inner critics . . .
Give each critic in your "gang" a name . . .

Here is a list of five inner critics adapted from the work of Internal Family Systems (IFS) psychologists Jay Earley and Bonnie Weiss.[14] I'll name each critic and then discuss its protective aspect.

The Perfectionist

This critic tries to protect you from exposing your shortcomings or making mistakes. It preempts criticism from others by wanting you to do things tip-top.

My psychotherapy client Rahm learned to name his Perfectionist. Rahm is a handsome, thirty-something man in the retail business. Each time he comes to a session, his hair is trimmed, shoes polished, and suit clean and crisp. I can almost feel the starch in his shirts crackle each time he shifts in the chair. He could be a model for *GQ* magazine. But when he makes a mistake or receives critical feedback, especially at work, he berates himself, ruthlessly picking on small errors. Needless to say, he has suffered from bouts of depression in the past.

One day I suggested that he let something he does at home or at work simply be "good enough."

Rahm said, "Everything in me is saying *no* to that. There's no such thing as 'good enough.' When you say *good enough,* I hear 'half-assed.' And half-assed is not acceptable."

Nothing would ever be good enough for Rahm, even when it was way above average for most people.

The inner critic that we'll call the Perfectionist:

- Sets high, inflexible standards for what you do.

- Has difficulty finishing a task or letting it go out unless it represents your absolute best work.

- Tries to make sure that you will not be judged harshly or rejected.

- Has expectations that probably reflect those of people who have been important to you in the past.

The Driver-Driver

This one is my internalized dá—*Old Joe,* the drill sergeant and taskmaster. The Driver-Driver doesn't want you to fail, so it pushes you to work hard and be successful.

Some years back, I was coloring with my youngest granddaughter, Olivia. Her dad is a hardworking man who splits each piece of wood in his sky-high woodpile by hand. It gives him "something to do" on the weekends.

Olivia was four years old and we had been sitting at the kitchen island, working on our coloring project for about forty-five minutes—an extraordinary amount of time for someone that young to concentrate on a task. We were coloring a large sheet of transparent paper with colored markers. It was going to be a stained glass window to hang in the window when we finished.

I was tiring and said, "Livie, how about if we take a break and have a snack? We can do some more tomorrow."

Livie, a tiny girl with beautiful blue eyes and long dark hair, was bent over the paper, still coloring. "No, Grandma," she said, "we're not finished! We have to keep going. I'm not a quitter! When I get tired, I just keep going!"

At that moment, she sounded just like her father.

The Driver-Driver:

- Fears that you may be mediocre or lazy.

- Fears that you will be judged a disappointment if it does not prod you to keep striving.

- Often pushes in a way that activates a procrastinator or a rebel to fight against its harsh directives.

The Persecutor

This critic attacks your fundamental self-worth, motivated by the belief that it might be safer for you to be invisible or not to exist. The Persecutor's voice might sound like this:

- How can you be so stupid?

- You could never do anything right!

- If you think it's so bad here, wait until you get out in the real world.

- How dumb are you!

- You've ruined my life.

- I wish you'd never been born.

- Oh! For God's sake.

- What do you want now?

A student in one of my meditation classes wrote this scenario about her Persecutor for a class assignment:

> I was getting my prescription bottles out so I could be ready to call the pharmacy for refills. My spouse was in the same room, watching me. She said, "How many medications do you take?"
>
> As I was counting, I said, "1-2-3-4-5-6. Six."
>
> She said, "I bet if you ate better you could be off some of those medications."
>
> Her remarks came across as an indirect way to tell me what to do, and I felt judged and shamed. I thought, "She's right. What the hell is wrong with me? I am such a fatso, too lazy to do anything about it. Nobody can care about someone like me. I don't deserve it."

The Persecutor shames you, making you feel inherently flawed and not entitled to basic understanding or respect. This most debilitating critic comes from early life deprivation or trauma. People who have been abused in childhood often have an internalized voice that is more harsh than that of their emotional, physical, or sexual abuser, forming "a vicious, scare-mongering inner critic." [15]

According to psychologist Donald E. Kalsched:

> The psychological system created when a child is traumatized is life-saving, but has a terrible downside. The normal reaction to unbearable pain is to withdraw from the cause of that pain; however, when we are children, and it is our caregivers who are causing pain, we cannot physically withdraw, so withdrawal happens at a psychological level instead. We dissociate. Our relational and creative potential . . . goes into hiding in the unconscious. At the same time, another part of the psyche moves to the forefront to become its protector. . . .
>
> . . . The inner protector becomes an unwitting inner persecutor. Healing requires that we move beyond the protector/persecutor, enter into our brokenness and reconnect to our buried potential, as well as to the original pain.[16]

Stay close . . .
Stay close to your inner critics . . .
Invite them in for tea . . .
   listen to them without judgment . . .
Stay close . . .

The Saboteur

This critic tries to squash you down. Its job is to undermine your self-confidence and self-esteem so you won't take risks. One of my clients described her inner Saboteur this way:

> I asked a friend to help me with my résumé. When I showed up at his house, I was wearing a crochet hat. He said, "Does that hat even keep you warm?" His comment angered me, but I didn't say anything.
>
> We sat down to work on my résumé, and he immediately started telling me what was wrong with it. I got super frustrated and just left his house.
>
> I felt like he was saying I was stupid . . . that I didn't even know how to dress for winter, for #####'s sake. When he proceeded to tell me all the things that were wrong with the layout of my résumé, I felt even more stupid and ashamed. All I heard was, *How have you ever gotten a job without my feedback?* I usually work hard to stay one step ahead of criticism, so I can avoid it—but not this time.
>
> Immediately, another thought came in to my mind: *You should know how to write a résumé already, anyway. What's the matter with you?*

Remember that the Saboteur:

- Makes direct attacks on your self-worth so that you will not take chances where you could be hurt or rejected.

- Sometimes attacks when you have needs. If you have been emotionally neglected in childhood, the mere fact of having a need is intertwined with shame.

- In an effort to prevent you from repeating a painful or traumatic experience, seeks to protect you by sabotaging opportunities or despairing about life in general.

- Fears your being too big or too visible and not being able to tolerate judgment or failure.

This inner critic can lead us down the slippery slope of addiction to medicate our pain or into a world of fantasy to avoid hurt.

Often, a Saboteur is a response to childhood neglect. In the psychological literature, this is increasingly considered a form of trauma. Neglect can happen when parents fail to forge emotional bonds with a child—for example, when parents are emotionally preoccupied with anxiety or grief or riddled with alcoholism. Even parents who provide children with basics such as food and shelter can practice this kind of neglect. In response, children feel shamed and believe that they are to blame for their parents' emotional distance.

Of course, this all happens unconsciously. For children, shaming themselves is less terrifying than accepting that their caregivers can't be counted on for comfort or connection. Again, in many cases, even *having* a need evokes shame. It may take a number of years for an emotionally neglected child to recover.

The Pseudo-Self

This critic tries to get you to fit into a certain mold based on standards held by society, your culture, or your family. Leona's story offers an example.

A fifty-something professional, Leona has a spark in her eye. And when she laughs at herself, it's with her whole belly as she slaps her knee. She is, in a word, delightful.

However, Leona has a well-developed Pseudo-Self. It developed during her childhood to protect Leona from getting yelled at and hit by her mother. Leona learned well to avoid trouble, but now her old coping mechanisms are causing trouble. She comes to psychotherapy because she experiences a great deal of stress and has difficulties in her relationships at work. She says:

> I don't know how to communicate with my supervisor and want to spend as little time in front of him as possible. Usually, I quickly tell him what I think he wants to hear so I can get out of there. On one hand, I want to be under the radar and be ignored and left alone. On the other hand, I resent it if I am not acknowledged or positively recognized. I feel that I cannot be authentic because if I am there is too much risk; I fabricate and do not tell the truth with others.

I don't really know how to work and count on other people, including work peers and other team members. In the past, I have either taken on too much or was unable to know how to reach out to others or to use available resources. I feel in general, including in the work setting, that I really have no frame of reference of what is okay to feel or say or how to assert myself. I become almost catatonic when given a task or a project to do.

As Leona's story demonstrates, the Pseudo-Self:

- Wants you to be liked and admired and to protect you from being abandoned, shamed, or rejected.
- Fears that the Rebel or the Free Spirit in you would act in ways that are unacceptable.
- Keeps you from being in touch with and expressing your true nature.

> *Stay close . . .*
> *Stay close to what provokes you . . .*
> *Stay close to your inner critics . . .*

. . . And Do Nothing

Through our meditations, we now have greater insight about the workings of our inner critics. We better understand their exact nature.

But what should we do about them? True to form, our inner critics are probably itching for self-improvement: *Let's get something going here! Make a plan already! Do something to get rid of these "bad" parts of me!*

Not so fast, counsels the ancient practice of mindfulness and meditation. In fact, the venerable Pema Chödrön says that constantly trying to change ourselves is actually an act of aggression.

Did she really say aggression? the inner critics ask. *Seriously? That's a strong word.* Yet once we view our inner critics and their self-improvement agenda as aggressors rather than bearers of the truth, we radically shift our relationship with them. Our self-critical thoughts start smelling like that stinky egg—not so appealing, not so believable.

Pema continues: "Only when we relate to ourselves without moralizing, without harshness, without deception, can we let go of harmful patterns."[17] Pressing, pushing, or cajoling ourselves usually yields—at best—temporary results. In contrast, research on self-compassion shows that people who *accept* their shortcomings and failures are the ones more likely to take steps to improve themselves.[18]

> *Stay close to your inner critics . . .*
> *Stay close . . . and . . .*
> *Do nothing . . .*

Stay close (and do nothing) suggests you give yourself kindness and compassion just as you are. Begin by doing nothing to improve!

What? Do nothing?

Yes. Instead of trying to change, give kindness to your overweight self, your lazy self, your crabby self, your angry self, your grieving self, your excessively critical self—all of you, without exception. As in the words of the Christian hymn from 1845:

> *Just as I am, without one plea . . .*
> *Just as I am, and waiting not,*
> *To rid my soul of one dark blot . . .*[19]

When we relax with ourselves, meditation becomes truly transformative. This is where we rest in the spaciousness of mind. We stay close to both the stories of our inner critics and their root beliefs and do nothing. We wrap ourselves in kindness before charging off to action. Doing nothing is actually doing something. In the words of psychologist Carl Rogers, "The curious paradox is that when I accept myself just as I am, then I can change."[20]

Sister Mary Sharon Riley, my spiritual director after my stay at Nada monastery, worked with me for years to slow down, deepen my spiritual life through contemplative prayer and meditation, and get used to this notion of doing nothing. More specifically, she introduced me to the world of meditating with icons—portraits of archetypal saints or divine figures. Legend has it that solitary hermits living in cave monasteries in Russia during the fourth century developed this practice as a means of connecting to the Divine. These ancient ones saw an icon as a portal between this world and the spiritual world. They contemplated the image and symbolism of an icon with a "prayerful, meditative heart," and in doing so experienced insight about spiritual "truths" as well as altered states of silence and wonder.

Some writers have described icon meditation as "Christian Yoga." The technique was originally passed down only through oral transmission and initiation—not unlike the Buddhist tradition of mindfulness slogans. Now this form of contemplation is available to us all.

So for now . . .
Stay close to your inner critics (and do nothing) . . .
Stay close . . . and . . .
Do nothing . . .
Just be . . . held in kindness and care . . .

Meditation with Madonna and Child as "Holder and Held"

Sister Mary Sharon Riley suggested I contemplate the icon of the Madonna and Child, sometimes called the Mother of Tenderness. There have been many versions of this image throughout the centuries.

In this meditation with Madonna and Child, we enter the image and imagine that we are each of the figures, one at a time. First, we merge with the Madonna and imagine holding our infant self, breathing kindness to the baby, vulnerable and needing. Next, we switch roles and become the baby, concentrating on receiving the love and care of the mother.

Interestingly, the focal point of the meditation is not in our thoughts but rather the sensation of the mother's skin touching the infant's face—cheek touching cheek. It may sound odd, but you can put your hand on your arm or your cheek during this meditation and actually feel the sensation of skin to skin, breathing loving-kindness through the pores of your skin. Alternately, you can use the "heart mudrā"[21] of placing your hand over your heart to transmit compassion to yourself.

For me, the breakthrough came in concentrating on this point. I could recall the tenderness of a baby or small child— the silky, velvet sensation of newborn skin and the smell of talc powder. Loving-kindness is transmitted through this sensation, through the pores of skin-to-skin, holding and being held. Absorbing love. Doing nothing but being.

In this meditation, we hold ourselves in pure loving care and let go of trying to fix anyone, including ourselves. We accept ourselves just as we are, all the unwanted parts of ourselves—nothing more, nothing less. When we "wrap our pain in the warm embrace of self-compassion,"[22] there is less room for the inner critics to reign, allowing more room for joy to arise. Radical compassion toward ourselves helps us to accept others as they are, too—all of *them*, both the good and the bad.

Try This:

1. *Sit and open to sensation.* Begin this loving-kindness meditation by noticing the sensations of yourself sitting in the

chair or on the cushion: the shape of your body, like a mountain, with the firm base and the balanced root, and an upright
spine. Close your eyes all the way or open them just a crack,
fixed on a spot.

2. *Let the stillness in the body calm the mind.* Let thoughts that
seem engaging or plaguing pass by, as if you were a mountain
watching the clouds in the sky pass by. Respond to strong
feelings and body sensations in the same way. Notice that
thoughts gather and morph into different shapes and from a
host of weather conditions. As the clouds pass through, you
simply sit like a mountain drawing its strength from a deeper
place. In short: *Breathing in—mountain; breathing out—calm.
Breathing in—mountain; breathing out—solid. Breathing in—
mountain; breathing out—still.*

3. *Become aware of the breath in the body and tune in to these
sensations as you breathe.* Notice how the belly expands
when you inhale and receive the life force of breath. Then
exhale with a slight elongation of the breath, letting go of all
you cannot control. Follow the out-breath with attention and
notice the slight pause right before the in-breath arrives. As
you notice this space between the breathing-in and breath-
ing-out, also become aware of the nano-pause between one
thought and another.

4. *Now, bring in an awareness of Big Mind.* This is the vastness of the sky, the beauty of the earth, the depth of the
sea. Imagine that you can join through your breathing with
a great stream of beings who support you through all of
time with their meditation practice. In this stream are all
of the most loving beings that you have ever known on the

planet—people and animals, great beings and small beings, holy beings and ordinary beings. Perhaps you can see their countenance and the radiance of their faces. As you join this stream of energy, a divine mind of loving-kindness connects to you through the beating of your heart.

5. *Now, imagine that you are holding an infant.* This is a tender, precious aspect of yourself that you can place close to your chest. Imagine the sensation of the tender, soft infant skin on your skin. Notice that you can feel the vulnerability of this small being against your chest, where your heart beats beneath. Focus on the sensation of skin—cheek-to-cheek—as you hold this baby self close to you. At this intimate point, you transmit loving-kindness to this baby-being-self.

6. *Breathe loving-kindness.* This little one, tender and vulnerable, is very dear to you. Through the pores of your skin and the rhythm of your breath, breathe in any hurt and need from the baby-self; breathe out an enveloping warmth. Stay with this practice for several breaths.

7. *Hold aspirations that the baby may be well.* In the next few breaths, return to the sensation of skin-to-skin, cheek-to-cheek. Notice the warmth of your heart and send loving-kindness to this baby-being. Wish that he or she feel safe in your arms. May her heart be happy and be filled with joy. May he be strong and healthy. May she have ease of well-being in this life.

8. *Next, imagine that you can change positions and let yourself become the baby.* Now it is you who is being held in the tender, skin-to-skin embrace of your loving caretaker. Let

yourself become the little baby-being that feels the warmth of her caretaker's skin, the strength of his body, the beat of her heart. Nestle in and receive loving-kindness, letting yourself be held and allowing the energy of kindness to come your way. As you breathe in, loving-kindness comes in through the pores of your skin, without effort, through divine osmosis. The caretaker hears your cries, knows about your sufferings, and wishes for you to be well. You are being swaddled in that energy. In the last several breaths of the meditation, focus on resting on the chest of this solid, strong, and kind source of love.

9. *Now, let all thoughts dissolve.* For the last few moments, bring your attention back to the belly, the solidness of the floor beneath you, the cushion holding you, and the sensation of breathing, resting in the openness of mind.

. . . (For now) . . . Stay close to your inner critics (and do nothing) . . .

4

Train in the Three Difficulties

Take a moment now to review the journey we've taken so far in this book. Our path to building a kinder voice traces the ancient map of *lojong*—mindfulness slogans for training the mind. We set our course with the first mantra, *Always train with slogans.* We then awoke to new possibilities by exploring the nature of change. Next, we created spaciousness around the busy mind with the slogan *Rest in the openness of mind.* Then we became deeply familiar with our inner critics, even naming them, as we *Stay close (and do nothing).* Like Buddha inviting Mara in for tea, we, too, have begun to befriend our enemies.

By now, I hope you are experiencing some of the power of working with mindfulness slogans in meditation—turning the phrases in your mind, perhaps writing them in your journal many times, steeping them in your inner mind. Have the slogans begun to whisper their wisdom to you—perhaps popping up in your mind unbidden, guiding a moment of angst to a more peaceful self-acceptance?

Let's continue. Once intimate with our inner critics, we can now take aim at the root of their power over us. We do this with our next slogan: *Train in the three difficulties.* This saying suggests a straightforward approach for what to do with our minds instead of feeding the stories of our inner critics or railing against them. The three aspects of this approach are to:

- Recognize the stories of our inner critics as soon as they arise.
- Be willing to do something different.
- Aspire to make the change a way of life—and repeat the process again and again and again.

Even though this approach presents difficulties, the underlying message of this slogan is one of comfort: You can train your mind and, as a result, wire it differently. You are not doomed. Inner critics need not have permanent residency.

> *Train in the three difficulties.*
> *Train . . .*
> *Train the mind . . .*

Training Makes the Difference

I know the value of this mindfulness slogan from my own experience and thirty-some years of working with people in clinical practice.

One of my personal stories is that I'm "chubby and uncoordinated." Dá used to compare each of us kids to the other growing up. My older sister was the athletic one, I was the "brainy" one, and my younger sister had the great personality. My brother was just "the boy," exempted from all household chores but taking out the trash. Characteristic of alcoholic families, our roles were rigidly cast.

Because athleticism had already been taken, I was seen as not having any. This led to ridicule for not being as physically graceful as my sister, who excelled at any physical challenge. She won tennis trophies, played basketball, rollerbladed, cross-country skied, and canoed. Me? I "ran like a girl" and kept dropping the ball when playing catch in the backyard. To which my dá said, "What the hell's the matter with you? Why can't you be like your sister? Any dummy can catch a ball." By the time I was ten years old, I withdrew from games with kids in the neighborhood and started reading books in my room. Alone.

Back in my day (the 1960s), every high school student had to complete the Presidential Physical Fitness Test as part of their physical education. In case those weren't your days, here's the context: Research in the 1950s showed that Americans were out of shape and in poor health compared to Europeans. The findings got President Dwight Eisenhower's attention and he formed the President's Council on Youth Fitness. Later, President John Kennedy upped the ante and created the Presidential Physical Fitness Test. If you passed, you got a very cool Presidential Physical Fitness Award badge to sew on your jean jacket.[1]

I failed, miserably, and got a "D+" in physical education that year. (*What is a D-plus anyway? A D is a D! It was a fail in my book.*) I would have been top in my class if not for that grade. It relegated me to salutatorian, and all I felt was bad that I should've done better.

Not so long ago, I told my granddaughter Julia about my *D* in phys-ed. She said, "How is that even *possible,* Grandma? Doesn't a person get a *C* just for showing up to gym class? I've never even met anyone who got a *D* in physical education." We both laughed until our sides ached.

Indeed, it's a funny story now. It wasn't then. I had so deeply internalized the shaming from my growing up that I couldn't do five push-ups at the age of fourteen. I hated gym class, didn't want to try any sport for fear of looking stupid, and came to believe that I was truly deficient in the coordination department.

It took until I was in my thirties and started taking ballroom dancing classes that I realized the story was a myth. I could dance! Not at first, of course. It took training and effort. I had a great teacher who encouraged me. I practiced, sometimes until my feet blistered. And then I won a few competitions. *The training worked.* The old story fell away.

Athletes have known for decades that training makes a difference. Some even say it makes for *most* of the difference when it comes to performance in sports. But the idea that we can train our minds for greater happiness is relatively new. Indeed, it was mind-blowing to me: *What? There are practices and tools for re-wiring the brain—for changing our emotional habits for the better? I'm not stuck with the propensities I acquired from early life? I'm not resigned to live with a harsh inner critic taking up residence in my mind?* Today I know that the answer to all these questions is yes.

One person who gains hope from these possibilities is my

client Bridger. He is a sweet young man, father of a new baby boy, and a recovering addict with a history of relapsing. His latest relapse to using drugs and drinking was a few months ago, shortly after his father's suicide. His father suffered from depression, his grandfather suffered from depression, and his great-grandfather suffered from depression. All of them committed suicide. Bridger suffers from depression and his inner critic is something fierce, prone to bouts of hopeless despair and immense frustration with the injustices of the world. He has a heavy, heavy legacy to overcome.

Bridger came to me to learn mindfulness for his depression. He sat in the brown leather chair in my office, tearing up. He has never had more than three months of sobriety and he was coming up on ninety days the following week.

"I feel like I am doomed," he said. "I don't want to be like my dad, but how can I be any different? Sometimes I feel like I just don't want to be here and it would be easier to just check out. But, I don't want to do to my son what my dad did to me. Can I really change how I am?"

My response was intense. I shared the story of one of my first Al-Anon meetings where people told me I could be happy in spite of my family. I talked about the research that says we can rewire our brains and etch new neuropathways for different and better emotional habits, even as adults. I cited findings about the plasticity of the adult brain. Then I said, "It won't be easy and it won't be fast, but you can do it if you are willing to train in mindfulness. It's like the Twelve Step program says: *Keep coming*

back. Keep coming back to the meditation cushion, mindfulness, the practices of mind-training. None of us are doomed!"

> *Train . . .*
> *Train . . .*
> *What does it mean to train the mind? . . .*

Training the mind for happiness is going to take work. Ancient meditation masters tell us through this slogan to "just do
it" if you want the benefits. Take radical responsibility for the
state of your mind and be willing to make an effort. Keep coming back to the mindfulness practice, to the meditation cushion,
to the present moment.

Who among us hasn't heard that "practice makes perfect"?
Athletes and musicians and dancers do it all the time. We accept
this adage without dispute when it comes to their areas of performance. And, the idea that practice is necessary has never been
a controversial concept in the scientific literature. In fact, a study
that looked at the performance ability of violinists showed that
the best musicians accumulated at least 10,000 hours of training.
Those classified as merely "good" or "least accomplished" were
found to have done only 8,000 or 5,000 hours of practice, respec-
tively.[2] Peter Keen, director of performance at United Kingdom
Sport, adds that it usually requires at least 10,000 hours of delib-
erate practice for an athlete to become elite.

Ten thousand hours is typically two to three hours of practice a day for eight to ten years of your life![3] That's amazing devotion. How can we expect that less is asked of us when training

the mind? How can there be any "softer, easier way" to train for an athletic pursuit? Or to achieve musical proficiency? Or to master a dance? Training the mind and re-wiring the brain is no less an effort, no less a "failure" when not achieved.

Inner critics don't go down easy. Still, we want them to. "Not enough time" is a refrain in our culture. The Dalai Lama says, "The problem in the West is people want enlightenment to be fast, to be easy, and if possible, cheap."[4] By cheap, I don't think the Dalai Lama means money. He means cheap in the sense of *You know, just meditate casually and it will work.*

I thought so, too, until doing an about-face some years ago. Rather than trying to tuck meditation time into my busy life— and failing—I decided to organize my life around my meditation practice. Now I often do it first thing in the morning, schedule it into my calendar, and let go of something else instead, like social media, TV, or even housecleaning. Many evenings, I turn off the computer at 9:00 to meditate. After years of practice, I am still unable to hold my intentions perfectly. Yet I'm practicing, putting in the hours, and reaping the benefits.

When it comes to seeing benefits from mindfulness training, we are not talking about anything close to the two to three hours a day required for elite athletes or performing artists. Research from Jon Kabat-Zinn's standard-bearing mindfulness-based stress reduction (MBSR) program at the University of Massachusetts General Hospital was based on meditating for forty-five minutes a day. And remember our earlier reference to Susan Lazar's work at Harvard? This research suggests that results were obtained from twenty-seven minutes a day of practice. Recently, the Penny George Institute for Health and Healing in Minnesota claimed benefits in reducing cigarette-smoking addiction with people who meditate for only *nine minutes a day.*

Biochemist turned Buddhist monk Matthieu Ricard says:

> You don't become a good pianist instantly; we're not born knowing how to read and write, everything comes through training, and what's wrong with that? Skills don't just pop up because you wish to be more compassionate or happier. It needs sustained application. But it's joy in the form of effort. Everybody who trains to do something, musicians, sportsmen and so on, says there's a sort of joy in their training, even if it seems to be harsh. So in that sense, it does take time. But why not spend time? We don't mind spending 15 years on education, why not the same to become a better human being?[5]

Indeed, there is joy in the effort of building a kinder voice.

> *Three difficulties . . .*
> *Use your difficulties to train the mind . . .*
> *Which difficulties?*
> *The first difficulty: Noting your critical "stories" as soon as they arise . . .*
> *Realize your critical "stories" are empty of real truth . . .*

See them as just a "neurosis" . . .

Recognize the Stories of Our Inner Critics as Soon as They Arise

We first practice noting the inner critic's stories on the spot, at the first instant they start up. The sooner we identify inner-critic-thoughts the better, since once we're in a downward spiral, the more emotionally overwhelming it becomes. Training to become aware of our "thoughts in the thoughts" can help us, over time, become more intimate with our mental narrative, more able to recognize self-loathing, self-shaming, or critical-of-others stories. We become intimate with the smell of that "stinky egg" in our mental refrigerator the moment it arises.

Further, we realize that the stories of our inner critics are learned, internalized mental formations—thoughts that may be "real but not true."[6] With practice, we learn to see through the delusions of our inner critics. Empty of truth, they are just the noise of "neurosis." In fact, meditation teacher Pema Chödrön actually offers this slogan as "Recognize a neurosis as a neurosis."

What does it mean to "recognize our neurosis as a neurosis"? Though the term *neurosis* is now a bit passé, it suggests that we should not take our stories all that seriously. Rather, see them as built upon a propensity to worry, to criticize when afraid, to be emotionally reactive to other people or situations. We can learn to see our stories as mental formations, incomplete understandings at best and rooted in insecurities and anxieties that are both conscious and unconscious. We learn, in fact, to accept the fact that most of us are neurotic some of the time. True, there is such a thing as a trait of neuroticism in some people. But Pema is referring to a more situation-specific neurosis—a maladaptive way that we adjust to our environment.

Had I had the advantage of mindfulness training, I could have perhaps discredited and let go of my story about being "chubby and uncoordinated" sooner. I could have seen it as a neurosis, simply noise, having no true substance. I could realize that it was just an idea about myself learned from the causes and conditions of my upbringing. Something real but not true.

The ability to notice neurosis as a neurosis requires considerable self-awareness. Because my inner critics are such familiar and constant companions, many times we don't recognize them. Their voice just seems like reality.

How, then, do we train in the first difficulty: learn to recognize our "neurotic stories" as soon as they arise? The training starts with the "awareness of the body in the body," as we talked about in chapter 2. A colleague talks about learning to sense the subtle shifts in his body, such as the soft feeling in his throat when he feels sad—the sensation a nanosecond before his inner critic steps in to "protect" him from feeling sorrow.

He learned how valuable it is to notice emotional triggers through mindfulness of the body, mindfulness of our feelings, and mindfulness of our thoughts. With sadness, for example, the brain seems to open a ZIP file that expands with content. We can go from feeling sad about the death of our cat to feeling sad about the death of other loved ones; to feeling sad about our relationship with our children or friends or family; to feeling critical of them for not being who we want them to be; to feeling shameful that there must be something wrong with us that they don't call more often or pay attention to us in the way that we want. Because of the way our brains are wired, our environment can easily trigger emotional associations from the past, or from our interpretation of past events.

Use Mindfulness to "See Your Neurosis as a Neurosis"

If we are able to observe with mindfulness, we can see when something is "up" emotionally and when one of our stories is activated. Following are some ways to use the breathing and noting mindfulness practice introduced in chapter 2 to specifically work with neuroses once activated.

Try This:

Breathe, and note your stories with a mental tag such as:

- This is just a shame-based story.

- This is just a toxic thought that comes out of my past.

- This is just a thought that arises because of my faulty brain wiring.

- This "story" is just an old habit.

- Oh, "Hi" [name your inner critic], I know you and watch the thought go by like a cloud passing in the sky.

- This is a mental habit that is not really helpful.

- These thoughts are just what I am making up about this person or situation.

- This is only a moment of suffering.
- Moments like this are part of life.

Train in the second difficulty . . .
Be willing to do something different . . .
Be entirely willing to let go of old, self-shaming beliefs . . .
Guard the mind from toxic thoughts . . .

Be Willing to Do Something Different

The second difficulty is taking action, training our minds in new habits; to "take corrective measures."[7] Here we are literally re-wiring our emotional patterns, etching new neural pathways with mindfulness and other therapeutic practices. With practice, we can create a new neural default, a different "go-to" response in the face of being triggered.

I love this story from Pico Iyer in his book, *The Art of Stillness,* and I think it is apropos to our discussion:

> I once went for my annual checkup with my doctor, and he said, "Well, your numbers are all fantastic, but you're getting on in years so you should spend thirty minutes every day in a health club." As soon as he said that, I signed up the next day, and I religiously, so to speak, observed that practice.
>
> But when another friend of mine asked me, "Have you ever thought of sitting still for thirty minutes

every day?" I said, "Oh no! I don't have time, especially now I'm on the treadmill for thirty minutes every day." Not beginning to think that of course the mental health club or just sitting still is much more essential to my well-being, my happiness, and probably even my physical health than the treadmill. And I think it so often happens that somebody says, "Change your life" and you repaint your car rather than rewire the engine.[8]

When we hear the ancient masters instruct us to train in the second difficulty, how many of us respond similarly, wanting to paint our car rather than rewire our mental engine? Do we resist letting go of a well-engrained habit of finding fault with ourselves or others?

Yet, this second difficulty asks us to really take full responsibility for our propensities, to notice them and take responsibility and decide: *Is this really how I want to live my life? Is this how I want to continue to interpret the world? Is this how I want to interpret other people's behavior?*

Not unlike Step Three in Alcoholics Anonymous,[9] we are asked to "*make a decision* to turn our lives and our will" to a spiritual path, to undermine our inner critics at their root, to see through the delusions of not being good enough in our eminently human state. Both the Twelve Step recovery program and the ancient practice of *lojong* remind us that we have a choice of where to place our attention, what attitudes to foster in our minds, and how to live out our lives. Buddhists call this taking *radical* responsibility for ourselves.

Okay—so what are some examples of "doing something different"? In Pema Chödrön's commentary on the second difficulty,[10] she tells us to "apply a technique or antidote to overcome the neurosis [of our inner critics]." Here we start actively re-wiring the brain for a kinder voice. And we can draw from both ancient mindfulness techniques and the more modern mindfulness and acceptance-based psychotherapies to do so.

Let's explore some of the possible techniques. Following are four fundamental mindfulness strategies for doing something different with the stories of our inner critics.

Dis-identify with Stories by Building Meta-Cognitive Awareness

Meta refers to *going beyond,* and *cognitive* means thinking. The essence of this strategy is to go beyond our thinking by stepping back from it and simply becoming aware of it.

Beverly experienced the power of this strategy. Sitting in her gray cubicle at her corporate job, she had dreamed of her next venture. In her mind, the picture was beautiful—giving elderly people who were dying comfort and care, actually making a difference in the world. To prepare for a mid-life transition into this new career, she finished her bachelor's degree and spent time volunteering at a hospice. She loved that work.

Soon after landing her ideal job, reality hit. The position wasn't really what she thought. Working with people in hospice was far more difficult than she had imagined. She also realized that she'd ignored red flags about the job while interviewing for the position.

Because of her mindfulness practice, Beverly soon realized that she had manufactured a story about what her new job and the people were going to be like. She saw that it wasn't really the job that was letting her down—it was the story she had constructed about what the job was *supposed* to be. She had seen only what she wanted to see. Once she backed off judging and criticizing her employer and co-workers, Beverly could see her own part in the disappointment. The story in her mind blinded her to reality. Realizing this freed her resentments.

Dis-Identify with your Stories— Build Meta-Cognitive Awareness

Try This:

- Observe your thoughts as they come and go, using *breathing and noting* practice. (After your meditation session, you could even map out the chain reaction of your thoughts and associations on paper.)

- Dis-identify with the critical stories by considering that thoughts and feelings are not facts, but rather passing phenomena—learned mental habits.

- Reflect, looking into the sources of your stories and inner critics. How did you learn this belief?

- Re-direct your attention to the here and now. Use your breath to come into the present moment awareness: feel your heart

beat, taste your tea, smell the roses, or listen to the sounds
of the birds.

- Remind yourself that you have more choices of how to see
the situation. Generate a list of at least three possible alternative interpretations.

Train in the second difficulty . . .
Build a toolkit of alternate practices . . .
Train in making loving choices toward yourself
    and others . . .

Cut the Mental Habit with a Practice

Jack had strong feelings about "fat people." He felt aversion. He
himself loved to eat but was judgmental about those who had
"let themselves go" and become obese. Whenever he took a walk
and passed by an overweight person, he noticed how critical his
thoughts became and the smug superiority he felt as he compared himself to "those people."

Once Jack began to train in the three difficulties, he became
aware of how often his mind was filled with such thoughts. He
decided to cut his judging habit with a practice of loving-kindness. As soon as he noticed his negative stories about overweight
people, he was determined to send them loving-kindness instead
with the slogan *May you be healthy, may you be well.* He noticed
that this new practice gave him a concrete alternative for what to
do with his mind and overall made him a happier person.

After a number of years of doing this practice, it became second nature to Jack. As he walked through the grocery store or went to a buffet restaurant, he sent some loving-kindness to every overweight person he met. He even relaxed with his judgments toward himself.

Cut the Mental Habit with a Practice

Here are a few possibilities for mindfulness-in-the-moment practices. You can do them in any moment to cut the mental habits of inner critics.

Try This:

- Do ten to fifteen minutes of walking meditation.

- Employ "pause practice"[11]—take three conscious breaths the moment you notice you are stuck in the voice of an inner critic. Slightly extend the out-breath as you exhale to calm yourself more deeply.

- Do a mini-body scan. Note sensations in your body that correspond with emotions such as jealousy, competitiveness, and worthlessness.[12]

- Dispute the "story" of your inner critic with compassionate, rational thinking.[13] For example, you could challenge:

  - "I must be crazy to feel this way" with *These feelings make sense in light of what I have been through.*

  - "I'm a bad person" with *I made bad choices.*

  - "I can't handle this situation" with *I have resources.*

  - "It's all my fault" with *It's probably 50 percent the other person's responsibility.*

- "I should know how to do this" with *I can learn.*

- Count your out-breaths down from 5 to 1. Do this as many times as you need to in order to redirect your attention.

- Turn a daily task into a moment of mindfulness. Such tasks include chopping carrots, doing laundry, or waiting in line at the grocery store.

- Recite the Serenity Prayer, a mindfulness slogan, piece of scripture, or stanza of poetry over and over again in your mind.

- Send the person you are judging some loving-kindness. Include yourself.

- Place a guardian at the gate of the mind—perhaps a religious figure from your faith tradition, a symbolic animal, or a person from contemporary culture that embodies a positive quality that you wish to evoke.

Train in the second difficulty . . .
Be willing to do something different . . .
Guard the mind from toxic thoughts . . .

Hold a Wide-Angle View

Our inner critics tend to simplify things: *The other person is an idiot or a selfish brat, or just lazy.* Instead of making quick judgments about a person or situation, mindfulness would have us consider the many causes and conditions that have led to this here-and-now moment. In the process, recognize that we may never be able to fully understand many of the influences in play.

Early in my career, I trained with the esteemed psychiatrist Carl Whitaker, the grandfather of family therapy in the United States in the 1960s. He had a provocative approach to psychotherapy, seeking to understand the "identified patient" in the context of at least three generations of his or her family. Dr. Whitaker treated the entire family system as the client rather than just the individual who came to him for help.

When Whitaker was working with an adolescent or adult, he'd gather several generations of family members for a session to explore the many conscious and unconscious influences in play. It was a wild and crazy ride to be in the room while he was at work. Yet Whitaker put whatever depression or anxiety or acting-out behavior was present in the client into a larger context. When seen through a wide-angle view, the client's issues began to make a certain kind of sense. Their symptoms may have been maladaptive, but seeing the larger picture made it possible to have greater understanding and compassion.

Similarly, we need to consider our inner critics in a wide-angle view. Perhaps, as we noted earlier, they started out trying to "help"—to protect us from some perceived harm. When I withdrew from sports as a preteen, for instance, I was shielding myself from the sting of ridicule. As a ten-year-old, I had no way of realizing that Irish families are notorious for shaming humor.[14] Nor did I have any memory of my grandfather's alcoholic cruelty, as he died before I was born. My father only told us that his dá was a great fellow with a rich baritone who liked to sing old ballads a cappella at the table after dinner. Not until traveling to Ireland as part of a family of origin project for graduate school did I hear the stories of my grandfather's raging temper and scrapes with the law. My dá was much like his own dá, especially after "having a few." He was carrying on the Stewart family legacy. All *I* knew was that I didn't want to drop the ball again when I played catch in the backyard. The humiliation burned. I made sense of my dá's shaming with a story that I was "chubby and uncoordinated," and that's why he was making fun of me. Why else would he do that? It must be my own fault.

All this became part of my wide-angle view. I saw how self-blame "protected" me from the pain of seeing my father's mean streak. I depended on him and my mother for survival. In addition, self-blame created an unconscious sense of mythical power in the situation. If *I* was the problem, then *I* could be the solution. I acted on this story by withdrawing—avoiding running around outside and playing games with the neighborhood kids, and, above all, tossing a ball in the backyard. This was my ten-year-old self's solution.

Perhaps many of our reactions to others, too, are based on a small view of the here-and-now moment. Often we are ignorant of other people's context. We have no picture of three generations of their family or cultural upbringing. We simply judge them.

Recently I facilitated a session with two sisters in different states via Skype. Their relationship had ruptured over their brother's drug use and subsequent legal problems. Both sisters were angry and critical of how the other had handled the situation. As we talked, each used harsh words to blame the other. One sister said, "I think [my sister] is just a mean person and I will never trust her again."

Yet there were many factors in play. Each sister felt scared by the situation. Each was horrified at their brother's crimes. Each had grown up in a household of yelling and blaming and shaming. One sister valued keeping confidences, and the other sister valued confrontation. They still don't see eye to eye, but through the sessions, each gained a wider view. Having a context helped the sisters come to more understanding of the other—some way to stay connected despite their differences.

My meditation teacher, the venerable Eigen Linda Ruth Cutts from the San Francisco Zen Center, advises me to contemplate the myriad causes and conditions that influence how members of my own family act: myriad conditions that led one of my sisters to cut herself off from the family; myriad generations of influence and illness that led to my father's violence and death from alcoholism; myriad causes and conditions that influence my stepchildren to keep their distance. There is always more going on than we can fully understand.

I wish I could simplify my family's situation into "good" and "bad," but it's far more complicated than that. I don't know about you, but I have found myself going through a list of slights while supposedly sitting in meditation. If I wrap myself in resentment about my sister, I'll just end up angry and not liking her. It's better for me to send her loving-kindness instead. It's better to hold my hand over my heart and think, *May you be relieved of your suffering so you cease to do harm. May you be happy.* I can hold a wide-angle view, acknowledge there is some kind of bigger picture, and realize that many conscious and unconscious influences are at work (in both me and the other person). In those moments, I am softened.

Mindfulness asks us to notice how resentments and inner critics affect our own state of mind. When I'm in judgment, it fuels anger; I feel tight and pessimistic. I find myself chewing on the grievances in my mind. Nursing my resentments doesn't enlighten the other person; the sole result is poison and unhappiness in my own heart. And if the other person picks up on the critical energy, it will make him or her defensive and reactive, too.

> *Train in the second difficulty . . .*
> *Be willing to do something different . . .*
> *Be entirely willing to let go of old,*
>   *self-shaming beliefs . . .*

Develop the Healing Practice of Self-Compassion

As much as we may be hardwired with the inner-critic patterns we have learned and internalized from early life experiences, "we also have a hardwired capacity to respond to our own suffering in a soothing, healing way—*self-compassion.*"[15]

Those words are from Kristin Neff, a developmental psychologist and student of Buddhist meditation. She defines self-compassion as having three main components: self-kindness, a sense of common humanity, and mindfulness: "*Self-kindness* entails being warm and friendly toward ourselves when things go wrong in our lives; *common humanity* recognizes the shared nature of suffering when difficult situations arise, rather than feeling desperately alone; and *mindfulness* [in this context] refers to the ability to be open to painful experience ('this hurts!') with nonreactive, balanced awareness."

These three aspects of self-compassion are precisely the opposite of our inner critics' reaction to internal threat. That reaction is based on self-criticism, self-isolation, and self-absorption.[16]

Psychological research shows that people who lack self-compassion are likely to have critical mothers, to come from dysfunctional families, and to display insecure attachment patterns. Childhood emotional abuse is associated with lower self-compassion, and individuals with low self-compassion experience more emotional distress and are more likely to abuse alcohol or make a serious suicide attempt. Research also indicates that self-compassion mediates the relationship between childhood maltreatment and later emotional dysregulation. This means that abused people with higher levels of self-compassion are better able to cope with upsetting events.[17]

This modern psychological view is aligned with ancient meditation, which teaches to do something different whenever our inner critics roar: *Be kind to yourself in the midst of pain.*

Train in the third difficulty:
   Make the "something different" a way of life . . .
Train in mindfulness . . .
Train in kindness and self-compassion . . .

Aspire to Make the Change a Way of Life—
And Repeat the Process *Again and Again and Again*

The third difficulty is that our inner critics keep coming back. It's hard to cut through them. Mind-training takes into account how we are all creatures of habit, shaped by our life experiences and conditioned to see reality in a certain way.

Pema Chödrön says the third training means "Have the determination not to follow the neurosis or continue to be attracted to it." Whether we want to or not, when we are young and vulnerable and dependent on the people around us, we take in and absorb their views and ways of seeing the world. This conditioning stays with us. It's easy to fall into our family ways because they are engrained in our unconscious. To choose a different way requires considerable self-awareness and effort.

In the third training we ask: *Is this view that I'm holding really true? What am I adding or projecting?* Through mindfulness practices, we come to see our propensity to judge ourselves and other people. Our view is necessarily limited and likely evidence of the way our mind tilts. By doing something different again and again and again, we create new neuropathways in the brain, etch new default patterns, and rewire our inner critics for the better.

This is the message of the third training: keep coming back to your intention; keep coming back to the practice of mindfulness. Ken McLeod, translator, author, and teacher of Tibetan Buddhism, says, "Be decisive in your attitude that such disturbances will never arise again." Keep coming back to your meditation seat; train again and again and again, claim small steps of progress, and rest in the openness of mind all the while. This moment is all we need to make progress, not more.

> *Train in the third difficulty:*
> *Aspire to make the change a way of life . . .*
> *Train again and again and again . . .*
> *Rewire the brain . . .*
>
> *. . . Train in the three difficulties . . .*

5

Begin Kindness Practice with Yourself

The beautiful slogan we'll explore in this chapter invites us to do something radical—to make kindness a way of life. And, we begin with a kinder voice toward *ourselves*. Eastern teachings are quite clear on this point. To love others, we begin with turning a kinder, gentler voice toward ourselves. Before planting the seeds of new thoughts to replace the voices of inner critics, we allow some space around those voices and send ourselves compassion. Only then, over time, can the new thoughts genuinely take hold.

His Holiness the Dalai Lama emphasizes that without knowing loving-kindness, there is no real basis for us to engage with others. Our efforts are likely to be rooted in our ego— wanting to do what other people expect, trying to act like a good person, fishing for praise, or the like. In the long run, we simply won't have enough inner resources to sustain being kind to others, especially if we are under stress or dealing with life's demands such as raising children, providing elder care, or coping with a difficult boss. We may run on empty, become depleted, or feel resentful. We're too pooped to pop.

The Buddhist story of King Pasenadi and his wife Mallikā illustrates this teaching. According to ancient lore, theirs was a great love story and a long, enduring marriage. They were known across the land for treating each other with kindness and respect.

One morning, the king and queen were discussing love over their chai tea. The king asked his wife: "Dear Mallikā, is there anyone dearer to you than yourself?"

"No, great king. There is no one dearer to me than myself. And what about you, great king? Is there anyone dearer to you than yourself?"

"No, Mallikā. There is no one dearer to me than myself."

Later that evening, the king sought out his spiritual teacher, Gautama Buddha. After greeting the Buddha, the king sat by his side and told him about his morning exchange with his wife. Upon realizing the significance of their understanding of love, the Blessed One is said to have exclaimed:

> *Searching all directions with one's awareness,*
> *One finds no one dearer than oneself.*
> *In the same way, others are fiercely dear to themselves.*
> *So one should not hurt others if one loves oneself.*[1]

Scholars interpret this verse to mean we are deserving of love and compassion—that no one else is more deserving, even if we searched the whole world. This view goes against the stream of ordinary culture, which values "humble bragging" at best. But the Eastern view is that there is no separation between ourselves and others. We wouldn't want to hurt another any more than we would want to hurt ourselves. We would wish for the happiness of others just as we wish for ourselves to be happy. In fact, there is no "other" to project our hatred upon—no "other" different from ourselves, no "us" and "them." There is only the great "We." We live in a universe of *interbeing*.

Our inner critics would have us think otherwise. We might treat others with kindness while holding criticism and contempt toward ourselves. In that case, however, we are still holding on to stories about "us" and "them" in our delusion of separateness. We become willing to do to ourselves what we would never do to others. We serve up harsh judgment, impatient demands, or undermining comments that we would never dream of directing toward another person, knowing the hurt that would be inflicted.

Still, our essential Self is of the nature of kindness. It's the entanglement of our stories and stalactite-like beliefs—now solid like stone—that have obscured our true, beautiful face. Mindfulness practice creates the space for us to see this as the stories and delusions of our inner critics. Loving-kindness practice allows us to touch our true nature once again and cultivate it to bloom.

> *Begin kindness practice with yourself . . .*
> *Begin kindness . . .*
> *Begin . . .*

Kindness Grows through Meditation

The good news is that the quality of kindness can be developed through meditation practice.

My client had searched the world for livelihood and love. In a session via Skype, she told me about the pinched-nerve in her neck and its debilitating pain. She had emotional pain, too, living abroad and in a significant relationship with a man in military service. He disappears from time to time when he is "under the radar" on a mission. She never knows when he'll be sent out, and he can't tell her.

Last week was one such time—only the second "disappearance" in the year they've been together but enough to rub her psychological soft spots. When she didn't hear from him for several days, she began to feel uneasy. His texts were few, and when they came, they were evasive. She escalated from anxious to angry in an instant, blasting him with a string of critical messages, each one uglier than the last:

- Where are you? Who are you with? Why aren't you getting in touch?
- You don't even care that my neck is killing me. You haven't asked how I am.
- I'm fine for sex and free concerts, but when I really need you, you aren't around.

Once her rage quelled, the fears set in:

- This is it, the beginning of the end. He's not into me as much as I am into him.

- This is his way of telling me that he's leaving me.
- Of course he's leaving me. I'm not sexy enough to keep him.
- I knew this would happen.
- I should prepare myself to be alone again.

When her boyfriend returned ten days later, he reassured her that he cared. He said he thought he told her these incidences would happen. Special assignments were part of his job, and he was on a mission to rescue a hostage who had been kidnapped by radicals. No, he couldn't tell her more. No, he couldn't use a code phrase to clue her in. She would need to get used to his work if she wants to be with him.

My client was soothed but later needed to make amends for her "crappy" text messages. Then, a few days later, she started panicking again when he was forty-five minutes late for their dinner date. She feared he wasn't coming at all.

In our psychotherapy session, my client realized more clearly that the anxiety lives *inside* her. Her boyfriend's behavior is merely triggering her fears. "Not that he doesn't have a part in the messed-up communication," she said, "but the root of the problem is *in me*."

Previously we had talked about her mother's addiction to pain medications and my client's childhood fears about "which mother, sane mother or stoned mother" would show up when she came home from school. That history, coupled with her father's unpredictable rage attacks at the dinner table and her mother's premature death, had affected her more than she wished.

The connections between her past fears and her here-and-now reactions were registering. In the past, she typically told herself that it was silly to be anxious. She pushed away her emotions and tried to over-exercise her fears away—hence, the pinched nerve in her neck. I was encouraging her instead to be kind toward her scared self, to befriend her fears.

We talked about building a sense of security from the inside-out and having less reliance on the attentions of her boyfriend, difficult as her situation with his missions may be. I recommended she over-exercise less and begin to meditate more, suggesting mindfulness and loving-kindness practice five days a week for twenty minutes a time.

> *Begin kindness practice with yourself . . .*
> *Begin . . .*
> *Begin . . . again and again . . .*

Moving from Mindfulness to Concentration

In beginning kindness practice with ourselves, we move away from pure mindfulness practice, which is based on observing the mind without judgment and coming back to the present moment time and again. Now we begin to incorporate a more active form of concentration meditation. Now we hold an intentional, directed thought. We *do* think about something, giving a job to the busy monkey-mind that randomly jumps from point to point.[2] We train ourselves to send kind and befriending thoughts toward ourselves, etching new neuropathways in our brains. We say a loving-kindness blessing and repeat it like a mantra, over and over again. In this way, over time, loving-kindness soaks into our mind, into the depths of heart and soul.

Put another way: Mindfulness helps us see how we are wired and perhaps become less judging about what we find. This practice begins inner transformation. Then we go deeper to plumb the depths of our mental habits. For this deeper level of change—releasing our inner critics and re-wiring our brain in new patterns—we add the practice of concentrated kindness and compassion. And in the process, we give ourselves the same care we'd give to a valued friend.

Hearing the Kind Voice of Another Person

Some of us need to incorporate the voice of another kind person to help us learn kindness for ourselves.

This was true for me after a seminar for helping profession-als that I led in St. Cloud, Minnesota. The seminar had gone well for the most part. However, local administrators had eaten the first ten minutes of my session with announcements, and I subsequently went over the allotted time. When the clock struck 4:30—the appointed time to end—people became restless and started walking out. Seeing their backs through the exit pricked my shame. I should have cut out some of my material and ended on time. It was a chronic problem of mine, and I knew it. In the car on the way home, critical thoughts rustled:

- They must not have liked the seminar.
- I must have been dull.
- I had too much material again.
- I should have known better.
- When will I ever learn?
- They'll never ask you to present again—and that's probably a good idea.

Just then, a mindfulness bell rang inside my mind. *You're being really hard on yourself! Nit-picking. What would it sound like if you were kind to yourself about your mistake instead?*

At that moment, the image of a dear colleague came into my mind. A longtime Zen priest and psychotherapist, his voice is gentle and his smile crinkles up his whole face. Insightful in a razor-sharp and deep way, he also laughs with abandon at his foibles and mistakes. I could hear his voice and feel the radiance of his countenance. He would have said: *It's okay. You're okay. The talk was probably good enough. You can let it go now. Think about what you want to do differently next time and then let it go.*

Just then, I was able to hold on to my colleague's voice in me. The knots loosened in my stomach and I could breathe better. The cold numbness in my chest subsided. *Ahhh . . . okay.* I made some mental notes about next time and began to sing in the car.

When I walked into our apartment that evening, my husband said, "How'd the talk go, honey?"

"Well, it wasn't perfect. Next time I'm going to cut some material. But, it was probably good enough" And I meant it.

That dry, hardened soil of my heart had loosened, now able to take in the nectar of love.

I didn't know about it then, but recent research has found that compassion practices such as this—generating a visual image of a compassionate figure who sends unconditional love— actually lower stress hormones such as cortisol in the body. As the "bad stuff" is decreased in the body, the "good stuff" is increased. Self-compassion has been shown to increase oxytocin, a hormone that fosters feelings of safety, generosity, and self-compassion.[3]

> *Begin the practice . . .*
> *Begin the practice of kindness . . .*
> *But, what exactly is loving-kindness?*

Loving-Kindness Is a Limitless Quality

Not to be confused with a Hallmark-card-feeling, loving-kindness is simply described in Eastern literature as the ability to befriend ourselves and others just as we are. This includes all aspects of ourselves, especially the unwanted parts—the crabby self, the intolerant self, the critical self, the scared self, and more.

Perhaps we fear that practicing loving-kindness toward ourselves will make us into an egoist or a narcissist. But, befriending ourselves actually begets greater compassion and tolerance for others. It's when we try too hard to be a good person by gritting our teeth that we run into trouble with the ego. Co-dependent resentment or exhaustion builds. We wonder why we haven't been appreciated more by others. (This brings to mind another mindfulness slogan: *Don't expect applause.)* By contrast, numerous meditation masters hold that *if you truly love yourself, you'll more easily love others.*

The practices in loving-kindness come from an ancient body of Tibetan Buddhist teachings called the *Brahma-viharas,* translated to mean the "Divine Abodes." These teachings say that there are four such Divine Abodes, or Sublime Attitudes: the qualities of loving-kindness, compassion, joy, and equanimity. Why are these considered divine and sublime? It is because each of these four qualities is the essence of our True Nature, the Divine Within. Each of these qualities is seen as sublime because they are spiritual in nature, "the great removers of tension, the great peace-makers in social conflict, and the great healers of wounds suffered in the struggle for existence."[4] We are instructed to begin with loving-kindness as the foundation for building greater compassion, joy, and equanimity.

Buddhist teachings suggest specific meditations to cultivate each of the four Sublime Attitudes. With practice they can become the abode (*vihara*) of our minds, a new default way of thinking and being. According to Nyanaponika Thera,[5] these four qualities can become "the mind's constant dwelling places where we feel 'at home'; they should not remain merely *places of rare and short visits, soon forgotten.*"[6]

The Blessed Ones didn't have the language of modern neuroscience, but they described the power of etching new neural pathways in the brain through spiritual practice. Ancient teachers have lent us tools for an amazing possibility: that we can rewire the mind's habitual thought to hold a kind-versus-critical response to ourselves and others. We can rewire our brain for kindness, building a new dwelling place for the mind.

Further, the four Divine Abodes are sometimes seen as a teaching about the "Four Limitless Qualities." Each of these qualities is considered a "boundless state" because "in their perfection and their true nature, they should not be narrowed by any limitation such as selective preferences or prejudices."[7] This means that our heart can grow beyond any bounds we can imagine. We but need to water the seeds of loving-kindness and the other sublime qualities and they will grow themselves.

Not unlike in nature. Say we want to grow tomatoes. We cultivate the soil and create the conditions conducive to producing fruit. But we do not actually *make* the tomatoes grow. They grow themselves once we fertilize and water and weed. Likewise, the four qualities of loving-kindness, compassion, joy, and equanimity grow themselves beyond what we can imagine if we but sit in meditation, become more mindful, and aspire to embody the aspect of our True Nature. The ancient teachings suggest that we but need to "incline our mind" in the direction of loving-kindness for it to take root and begin to grow, even if we cannot feel any immediate result. Loving-kindness will grow itself, as nature grows a seed of flowers or plants, if we but provide the conditions.

Upon hearing these teachings, I thought, *Are you kidding? Sign me up!* I had no idea that it was possible to train the mind for happiness, to overcome the conditioning I had received from my upbringing; that there were specific "mind trainings" meditations to apply to cultivate these four qualities, beginning with loving-kindness.

The meditations for developing loving-kindness and the other Limitless Qualities are called the *Brahma-vihara-bhavanas*—the meditative development of these states. Nyanaponika Thera suggests that our minds become "thoroughly saturated" by them as guides to daily behavior, reflection, and meditation.[8]

The *Metta Sutta*, the *Song of Loving-Kindness*, tells us to practice kindness as an active, daily activity. And the venerable Thích Nhất Hạnh says, "In Buddhist teaching, it's clear that to love oneself is the foundation of the love of other people. Love is a practice. Love is truly a practice."[9]

> *Practice . . .*
> *Practice loving-kindness . . .*
> *How do we practice loving-kindness? . . .*

Again, the non-dualistic stance of Eastern practice is that we accept ourselves just as we are *and* yet be free of our harmful emotional habits. We hold both aspirations, often in the same breath. With the light of mindfulness, we see that our inner critics are not kind. Yet we desire to be more kind, more loving toward ourselves and others.

There is tension between these two awarenesses. Even so, we are not aggressively trying to improve ourselves with our willpower by setting goals or reciting affirmations. Instead, we are fostering conscious contact with our true Self, the Great Reality Within. Since our essential Self is of the nature of loving-kindness, our job is to simply water the seeds of that quality with our attention and aspiration. The limitless nature of the quality then grows itself. We provide the fundamental conditions; we don't actually do the growing itself. That, as the Twelve Step tradition reminds us, is the work of a Power much greater than ourselves.

When we aspire, we contemplate that a greater kindness can come to pass rather than ask for a magical result. Meditation crystalizes our intention, drawing in the necessary and supporting factors that are needed to manifest kindness in our lives. Aspiration practice helps us truly *want* to develop a kind heart and not just keep thinking we *should* develop a kind heart. Through meditation, we breathe oxygen into the flame of our desire for loving-kindness.

Practicing Loving-Kindness

So how else do we practice loving-kindness meditation? Formal loving-kindness meditation (*metta bhavana*) uses mental recitation to encourage and expand our desire to grow the quality. We repeat a four-line stanza time and again in our mind, soaking it into our consciousness, absorbing it into our bones, holding our desire with our power of intention. A contemporary translation of the four lines offered by Sharon Salzberg in her book *Loving-Kindness: The Revolutionary Art of Happiness* suggests these lines for meditation:

May I feel safe,
May I be happy,
May I be healthy,
May I live with ease.[10]

Notice that each line in the meditation begins with the words "May I." This poetic structure uses an age-old, rhythmic pattern of call-and-response found in both Judeo-Christian and Buddhist scriptures. In Biblical texts such as the Book of Ruth and Psalms of David, we hear people call to God. In the next verse, we hear God's response.

The Buddhist teaching is that there must be a response when we call out. Why? Because we are part of the great web of interbeing. There cannot *not* be a response. Hindu and Buddhist mythologies use the metaphor of Indra's web to depict this interdependency. In Eastern lore, Indra is the Vedic god of all creation. In his web, each of us is a jewel connected to all other jewels with threads of energy. If one part of the web is tugged, a tremor is felt in all the other parts. The whole web moves. We're calling to the energy of loving-kindness in the universe when we recite these blessings. We're saying, *Hey, remember me? Over here. Come my way!*

However, we're not calling to a being or an entity outside ourselves. Buddhism holds that when we call out, we're raising the energy inside ourselves. We're saying, "May loving-kindness arise in me. May it grow itself in me. May I have conscious contact with the Great Reality within, without, and between." Once the seeds of loving-kindness are watered in our consciousness, the quality grows exponentially, in immeasurable ways.

As you work with loving-kindness meditation, allow that many reactions are possible. Some people experience deep joy as their heart opens. Others touch the sorrow of not having known loving-kindness in their lives. Others seem dry, not feeling much of anything one way or the other. Remember that every such experience just *is;* it is neither good nor bad. None of them mean you are doing the meditation incorrectly. The teaching says that all we need to do is incline our mind in the *direction* of loving-kindness for the quality to take root. We need not feel sweet emotions right away. We simply keep watering the seeds of this beautiful quality with our aspiration.

> *Practice loving-kindness . . .*
> *Begin with yourself . . .*
> *Then expand kindness to others . . . and all beings . . .*

Begin with yourself in meditation, but never end there, with yourself as the entire focus. Take a moment at the end of your sitting to extend the aspiration toward others—people struggling with inner critics, "like me," people who are suffering with fear or shame in this moment, other parents, other sisters. May *they* experience loving-kindness. And then, one more expansion of loving-kindness in your final out-breath to all beings that are suffering. May *all beings* experience the healing of loving-kindness.

Loving-Kindness Meditation
("Metta Bhavana")

There are three parts to using mental recitation in loving-kindness practice.

Try This:

- *First, contemplate the four-line stanza of loving-kindness aspirations.* Recite each phrase slowly and silently in your mind, at least three times:

> *May I feel safe,*
> *May I be happy,*
> *May I be healthy,*
> *May I live with ease.*[11]

- *Second, stay with a line that calls to you and work with it more deeply.* Some people are drawn to a particular aspiration in that stanza of four. They may choose to work with that one phrase, steeping it in meditation for six months or a year. Another possibility is that you feel resistance to one of the aspirations. Maybe you feel angry when you hear it. Or, sadness wells up. Or, it seems confusing. If that's the case, there is something happening in the resistance. It's "got juice." Stay with it . . . choose *that* aspiration to work with more deeply.

- *Third, direct loving-kindness energy toward a specific difficulty.* You can linger on one of the aspirations, streaming loving-kindness toward a personal need.

For example, the first line, "May I *feel* safe," is an adaptation offered by Sylvia Boorstein, founding teacher of Spirit Rock Meditation Center in California. The traditional interpretation of this line has been "May I be safe, from within and without." Ms. Boorstein gives us this subtle but powerful shift to *feel safe*—something those of us raised with trauma have rarely or never felt. Many of the stories held by our inner critics have been born from the causes and conditions of fear or uncertainty or shame. Here ask for help to experience "being safe to be myself," relieving the mind of its anguish.

If you notice, as you grow in mindfulness, that your mind tilts in the direction of your inner critics—toward self or others—you may want to add a personalized aspiration. Examples include "May I be free of mental torments," "May I be relieved of shame," and "May I realize the delusion of my stories." While you linger here, stream loving-kindness to the agitations of your mind.

As you repeat the second line, "May I be happy," send loving-kindness to your heart and your emotions—each of your sorrows, hurts, or resentments. Ask that you be healed. Here we aspire to more than a relief from distressing emotions. The classical translation is: "May I be happy and never be separated from the source of true happiness." We are asking to recognize what actually makes us happy. That happiness is not present in the perfectionism or zero-tolerance-for-mistakes that our inner critics promote. We may find that as we do this meditation, our understanding of happiness shifts and our desires may change.

With the third line, send loving-kindness to your body. You can stream loving-kindness toward a particular habit or discomfort in your body as you say, "May I be healthy." You can think, "May I treat this precious body with kindness" or "May I be patient and friendly with this physical difficulty." It's not uncommon to have health problems if you are in a constant state of negativity brought on by inner critics, as the mind-body may manifest in symptoms (tension headaches, knots in the stomach, lower back pain). If so, working with this phrase in meditation can be of great benefit.

Or perhaps you have trouble caring for yourself physical-ly. You might be re-enacting neglectful family patterns such as burning the candle at both ends, forgetting to eat, or failing to exercise. Sending loving-kindness energy toward the struggle may help it change.

The fourth aspiration directs loving-kindness toward diffi-cult circumstances in your life. If you are in a life situation that's troublesome, work with the last line, "May I live with ease." Hold this aspiration in your mind. Send loving-kindness to the difficult circumstance, such as a relationship with your spouse, friend, or co-worker. If you are tight with inner criticism toward yourself or others, you could hold the aspiration, "May I ease up. May I open up! May I let go of what I can't control."

Another Loving-Kindness Training—
Tonglen, the Compassion Breath

Now that we have aspired to strengthen our heart and used mental recitation of phrases to grow our loving-kindness, we can go beyond words and thoughts in the practice of compassion breath.

The literal translation of the mindfulness slogan *Begin loving-kindness practice with yourself* actually reads *Begin sending and receiving practice with yourself.* The ancients here refer to a loving-kindness practice called "compassion breathing" or *tonglen.* This is a Tibetan word meaning "sending and receiving." This beautiful heart-practice originated in India and came to Tibet in the eleventh century. (Some contemporary writers have suggested this practice should more accurately be called *lentong,* or "receiving and sending," because of how compassion breath is actually practiced.)

Tonglen meditation is meant specifically for developing compassion, the willingness to feel and care about our own pain and the willingness to feel another's pain as our own. The practice is to not run away—to not try to convert the unfixable to the fixable by ascribing blame to ourselves or others and holding a co-dependent idea of mythical power.

Mindfulness sees the delusion of our inner critics. It recognizes the stinkiness of thoughts such as *If only my bangs weren't so ugly, those boys wouldn't be mean to me. . . . If only I achieve more, I'll be worthy. . . . I don't deserve a more loving relationship; this one is the best I'll ever get. . . . If I'm honest, I'll get blasted.*

Upon hearing these thoughts, compassion leans in and says, *I care about your pain. I can't necessarily fix it, but I care.* Whatever the nature of our emotional pain, says Pema Chödrön, in *tonglen* we "breathe in the desire to accept [the experience of life] . . . feel it, accept it, and own it, free of any resistance."[12]

Very simply, with our in-breath we say yes to our suffering from inner critics and *receive* it into our heart. We allow the suffering to be absorbed through our body and into the arms of our Big Mind or Higher Power, which is depicted as the vastness of the sky. On the out-breath, we let this Big Mind *send* relief and compassion through us and within us. We do this practice time and again until our suffering is transmuted. We can later do this practice for the suffering of others, yet the instruction is very clear: Begin sending and receiving (or, if you prefer, receiving and sending) with yourself.

Because *tonglen* works with the very breath itself, it reminds me of the admonition instruction to "pray without ceasing" in the Christian scriptures. Indeed, we are breathing at all times. This means that we can use our mindfulness to practice kindness and compassion toward ourselves—and ultimately toward others and all beings.

On a practical level, this practice turns the channel on our mental dial to a new station and gives the monkey-mind something new to do. Once the mindfulness bell rings in our consciousness, we can turn our attention to compassion breathing instead of critical thoughts. We bump our neurons off that well-worn track to a new way of being in the world. *Tonglen* practice helps us accomplish this training of the mind for greater happiness.

An important aspect of this practice is allowing suffering to be absorbed through the heart center and into the vastness of the sky—into the Big Mind of a Higher Power. Not many meditation teachers present compassion breathing in this way, but it has been a significant aspect to me personally.

I recall a vivid moment in my psychotherapy office in St. Paul, Minnesota, while listening to a client's story of profound abuse and suffering. I thought, *Oh, my God, I don't know if I can stand to hear this; I don't know if I can stay present; it's too painful.* In that moment, I was relying on my own powers to bear the unbearable, and it was too much.

I started to do *tonglen* breathing for my client. I couldn't think of anything else to do since no words would suffice. After some moments of breathing in the suffering, feeling my body brace against it, thoughts arose saying, *No! I don't want to hear this—I can't stand it. Get me out of here!*

In the next moment, the thought came, *You don't need to stand it! Of course you aren't strong enough or big enough. You don't need to be. The vastness of the sky is big enough to bear this.* I knew this to be true. The sky is vast indeed. I could let the emotional pain go through my body and mix with the molecules of the sky. The pain lightened. It mixed with the bigness of the sky and was diluted.

I thought, *The vastness of the sky and Creation is surely bigger than I am. I don't need to hold this being's pain in myself and by myself. Sky is big enough to bear it. Big Mind is vast enough to bear it.* Higher Power is big enough to hold what is unbearable. On the in-breath, I could breathe the suffering of my client into the vastness of the sky. On the out-breath, I can let compassion and relief be breathed through me.

My clinical work has never been the same, thanks to *tonglen* compassion practice.

Compassion Meditation for Yourself

Try This:

- As you sit in meditation, imagine that your True Self is the aspect of you sitting on your meditation cushion or chair. This is yourself as the embodiment of enlightened compassion. Directly in front of you is the ordinary aspect of you that suffers from inner critics, perhaps feeling shameful, fearful, stupid, or misunderstood.

- As you contemplate your ordinary self, imagine a warmth and tenderness toward your suffering. Your awareness opens your heart and generates a wish to release your inner critics.

- Consider that the suffering of the ordinary you takes the shape of a dark, smoky cloud. With each in-breath, visualize that you breathe in the cloud. As the cloud of suffering enters your being, imagine that it goes through your heart and body. Without any effort on your part the cloud of suffering gets absorbed through the breath into the vastness of the sky. Notice that Big Mind has the vastness to hold your suffering,

---

and that with your in-breath, the sky's lightness and space dilute the smoky gray cloud of your suffering. As the cloud of suffering gets subsumed into the molecules of the sky, it disintegrates the traces of clinging or fear in your heart, and reveals your essential Self—a radiant core of wisdom and compassion, which shines out even more powerfully, like a brilliantly shining sun.

- As you exhale, freely give out relief in the form of a color or texture or light in your breath. Bring relief and unconditional kindness to the suffering aspect of you. Continue this giving and receiving with each breath for as long as you like.

- As you continue the practice, visualize the ordinary aspect of you is gradually relieved of suffering and filled with a sense of safety and well-being. Each time you end the *tonglen* meditation, consider that the practice has taken hold: the ordinary aspect of you has released your critical thoughts or beliefs, and now holds greater self-acceptance. And, since there is no actual difference now between these two aspects of you, dissolve the visualization and remain in meditation.

Tonglen *on the Spot*

In addition to doing compassion breathing during our more formal sitting practice, we can do *tonglen* right on the spot at any time. In a moment when we feel emotional discomfort or bump into our inner critics, we open our heart and welcome the sensations with our in-breath. Then we send relief and comfort on the out-breath. In an instant in time, with a simple in-and-out breath, we can pause and send ourselves compassion.

Not long ago, I had such a moment while at the movies. After we purchased our tickets and went to get refreshments, I noticed my tight body and impatience with the popcorn guy. I wasn't aware of anything in particular that was bothering me; the day had been pleasant enough.

I said to Jim, "I feel so crabby I can hardly stand myself. I've been really edgy and short-tempered all day. I don't understand why!" (Inner voice: *Maybe you're just not a very nice person.*)

Jim looked over at my face and in his quiet and gentle way said, "When I'm like that, a lot of times it's because I'm grieving and I don't want to admit it."

Sometimes it's good to be married to another psychotherapist. At his words, I burst into tears. I realized that I was feeling lonely for our littlest granddaughter, who had just started kindergarten the week before. She was the last of three granddaughters, and the end of fourteen years of babysitting a sweetheart one day a week. I missed her. It was the end of a chapter of life. I was sad. Glad but sad.

Anywhere we are, however we are, we can do compassion breathing for ourselves, on the spot: breathing in the sharpness of our inner critics, allowing the negativity or shame to be absorbed into the vastness of Big Mind; breathing out, offering the heartfelt radiance of acceptance, loving-kindness, and compassion.

If we encounter someone else in pain, we can also begin to breathe in his or her difficulty and send out some relief. This is similar to the way we practice with ourselves. Even if there is no other way to help, we can always do compassion breathing for the other person.

Tonglen has been a powerful and relieving practice to help me stay present with loved ones who are suffering, such as the active addicts in my family and my mother as she aged and declined in health. Loving-kindness *can* become a way of life, a path to universal compassion. And it begins with ourselves.

> *Breathing in, right now, I'm cross . . .*
> *Breathing in, right now, I'm angry . . .*
> *Breathing in, right now, I'm grieving*
>   *beneath my anger . . .*
> *Breathing in, right now, I'm shameful*
>   *that I'm grieving . . .*
> *Breathing in, right now, I am not alone . . .*

> *. . . Begin kindness practice with yourself . . .*

6

There's Only One Point

There's only one point.
One fundamental thing ...
One ...

Now we are given our last mindfulness slogan to contemplate: *There's only one point.* Pema Chödrön puts it like this: "All the teachings and practices are just about *one thing:* if the way that we protect ourselves is strong, then suffering is really strong, too. If the ego or the cocoon starts getting lighter, then suffering is lighter, too."[1]

When we worked with the slogan *Stay close and do nothing,* we looked at the nature of our inner critics. We saw that they often arise out of efforts to shield us from hurt or harm. Their job is to protect the heart's tenderness. And yet we soon discover that our critics shrink our world to make our experience smaller —more fixated on *me: Am I good enough? Are my teeth straight enough or white enough? Did I sound stupid? Does she like me?*

Life is not as much about us as our inner critics would have us believe. Too much self-concern brings on deeper suffering, perhaps originating with a childlike part of us that implores, *What about meeee?*

The Many Flavors of Self-Centered Suffering

Just above the roster of arrivals and departures, the giant railway clock ticked 9:55 on a Friday morning. My friend held her four-year-old son's hand tight, making a beeline to the platform where their cousin was due to arrive from New York. They were running a little late.

"Come on, Máté, we have to hurry. Let's go! We don't want to be late. We need to be there when Lisa gets off the train. We don't want her to wonder where we are. Come on now."

The more she urged him, the slower he seemed to go. Abruptly, Máté pulled his little hand out of his mother's grip and dug in. Stopped in the middle of the concourse, glaring at her with his beautiful brown eyes.

Two paces ahead by now, my friend turned to her son. "What?"

"But, Mom, I am the only one!"

That's what the inner four-year-old in me still believes, too.

The suffering of *I am the only one* comes in many flavors: braggadocio, self-scrutiny, discontent, or resentment, to name a few.

Let's consider braggadocio for a moment. There is consensus among psychologists that a healthy self-esteem or positive ego strength is desirable; it can be good for one's mental health and mitigate anxiety or depression. However, recent research suggests that there's a problem with *how* people try to boost their ego and self-esteem—by comparing themselves in areas like physical attractiveness or successful performances or putting other people down to puff up their own value. Indeed, these propensities "may result in narcissism, prejudice, and bullying."[2]

Buddhists refer to such braggadocio as an attitude of excessive self-cherishing. This is not a self-valuing born from loving-kindness. Rather, it's an attitude that arises from hubris and denial, a belief that we are separate and better than others.

By contrast, greater kindness and compassion for ourselves does not generate narcissism. Research indicates that self-compassion is associated with *lower* levels of social comparison, self-consciousness, mental rumination, and anger.[3]

Then, too, our inner critics can generate another, sneakier form of self-concern: excessive self-scrutiny. A preoccupation with self, whether it is related to how great we are or how flawed we are, shrinks our world. We can find ourselves overly concerned with what other people are thinking of us, how stupid we sounded, or whether the people at the party liked the birthday cake we baked.

A few months ago, I led a retreat in Pennsylvania for women in recovery. They were a lovely group of vibrant, honest individuals. Several people commented on how recovery from alcoholism and other addictions had helped them be far less worried about their flaws, less harsh, and less critical in their self-talk. One woman said to me, "Before recovery, I was constantly preoccupied with what people thought of me, scanning for what kind of impression I was making; watching myself with a disparaging eye. I wasn't able to listen to others because I was busy planning what I was going to say back. I was too self-conscious and self-critical to be present." This is suffering, too—being burdened by concerns about self and not really present to life.

> *There's only one point . . .*
> *One . . .*
> *I am not the only one . . .*

Inner Critics Make Our "Bad Too Big"

The patient was a misfit for my afternoon group, and I knew it from the get-go. The clinic administrators assigned a man with sexual addiction to my psychotherapy group. Several other members were women who had been raped or were victims of incest. The mix was bound to be explosive.

I protested to the clinic supervisor, and she dismissed my concerns, "Sorry, that's the only time this patient can come in, so make it work!" (Translation: *We need the business.*) I was furious.

That day's group session was intense. It did not go well. Predictably, the women in the group who had been sexually abused were upset by the new patient's story of his sexual compulsivity. They said they would likely have trouble trusting him, at least for a good while. In response, he was defensive and self-pitying.

Then again, given the mix of people, I thought it could have been much worse.

That evening, the patient called his referring therapist to complain, telling him that his group therapist was "horrible" and that the other group members had been "mean to him." The referring therapist, angry and protective of his patient, called the head of the clinic to complain.

The clinic director came into my office the following morning and chewed me out for not facilitating more skillfully. I reminded her that I had asked that the patient be reassigned to a different group, and that the mix was a disaster-waiting-to-happen that no amount of skill could have prevented. The clinic director said, "Oh." She would look into the situation. But she did not agree to transfer the new patient to a more fitting group.

Even more furious, I called the referring therapist, whom I knew—although not well—and gave him an earful. I told him about my efforts to get the patient reassigned. I said I thought the women in the group had handled themselves relatively well— better in fact, than his patient. I was angry that he hadn't called to gain my perspective before complaining to the higher-ups. There was a long pause at the end of my diatribe.

Then he said, "I think you make a good point," and apologized.

I appreciated the apology, but was still miffed. Facilitating that group was one of the more difficult things I have had to do in my career, and I was a relatively young therapist at the time. The administration never did agree to transfer the patient. But somehow, over the course of the next twelve weeks, six women with abuse in their history and the one man with sexual compulsivity worked to heal themselves in my group. The women came to realize that he was a human who had been damaged and hurt, too, and who felt regret for his wrongs. The man began to realize the pain sexual acting-out caused others.

When the patient completed the program, the referring therapist attended the "graduation" ceremony. I caught a glimpse of him on the other side of the conference room. This was the first time I had seen him since our conflicted phone call. My pride was still smarting from the whole sequence of the patient's care. There had been no "congratulations, you did good work in a tough situation" from either my supervisors or the referring therapist. So, in an infinitely mature moment, I decided to snub him—not greet him, not go over to chat, not acknowledge the decency of his earlier apology. I turned and walked away.

The next morning, over coffee and the newspaper, I felt a bit embarrassed about my behavior, realizing it wasn't very nice. I considered sending the referring therapist a quick apology by email but discarded the idea. *Too much drama*, I thought. *But, next time I see him, I'll make sure to go out of my way to be friendly.*

As fate would have it, he walked into the coffee shop a few moments later. Unbeknownst to me, his office was upstairs. I gave a big greeting and we talked for a moment.

He said, "How about lunch sometime soon?"

Still a bit reluctantly, I said, "Okay."

Over that lunch a few weeks later, I mentioned feeling bad about snubbing him at the infamous patient's graduation.

He said, "You did? You snubbed me? I didn't even notice!"

(That referring therapist is now my dear husband, Jim.)

When our inner critics make our bad too big, we're in delusion—not present for our appointment with life. We're living in our inner house with the windows closed and the shades pulled while in reality the sun is shining and the sky is blue.

His Holiness the Dalai Lama says that too much self-scrutiny not only shrinks our emotional world, it hurts our health, too: "People who have the tendency to use more self-referential terms (*I, me, myself*) tend to have more health problems and earlier deaths. Being self-absorbed has an immediate effect of narrowing one's focus and blurring one's vision."[4]

By contrast, self-compassionate individuals tend to use more connected language when they describe their weaknesses. Researchers Neff, Kirkpatrick, and Rude found that self-compassionate people used "fewer first-person singular pronouns such as I, [used] more first-person plural pronouns such as we, and [made] more social references to friends, family, and other humans."[5] These results suggest that, when we feel more connected to the universal human condition, our personal weaknesses are not as big and become less threatening. In turn, we feel less anxious about our flaws and shortcomings. We're less alone.

People with more self-compassion ruminate less. This matters because rumination—mentally dwelling on our flaws—is a factor highly correlated with depression and anxiety. We can break the cycle of negativity by accepting our human imperfection with kindness.

There's only one point . . .
One . . .
The cocoon of ego causes suffering.

Inner Critics Foster Dissatisfaction with Others

Besides braggadocio and intense self-scrutiny, another "flavor"
from our I'm-the-only-one list above is resentment.

My client, without children of her own, relished her special
role of "Auntie" to her nieces and nephews. But today, as she
sat in my office, she was disgusted. The previous week, she had
asked her oldest niece if she would help serve hors d'oeuvres at
her annual garden party. Her niece declined with an imperial
nod, saying, "Sorry, that's not something I'm up for."

"What an entitled little twit!" the aunt exclaimed. "It's not
like I ask her many favors. It's usually me doing for her. Talk
about selfish!"

For the most part, her niece was a bright, lovely young woman and they shared many sweet times together. This incident
was one of the few significant conflicts in their relationship.

While meditating, my client noticed that her monkey-mind
was often judging her niece. In addition, her body held a low-
level ache and her mood was edgy. Little things bothered her,
not unlike when she was overly tired. Small tasks were more of a
challenge. She felt critical not only of her niece but also of many
other people, too, like the barista at the coffee shop and the bag
boys at the grocery store.

She said, "Even though I know better in my brain, it feels like my niece's selfishness is a rejection of me." When I asked her what it felt like to be in resentment, she said, "I feel tight, like there is a small part of my heart that's hard—like a stone."

After our discussion, my client decided that the next time critical thoughts came up about her niece, she would stop feeding them and send her niece a loving-kindness prayer: *May she experience loving-kindness and grow into generosity.* In the meanwhile, my client was the one who began to feel relief. She stopped taking her niece's "no" personally, and that lessened her shame and anger. She meditated with the phrase "Harden not my heart" from Psalm 95:8 and it soothed her critical thoughts. Maybe her meditations will even affect her niece in a positive way. It can't possibly hurt.

> *There's only one point: "Don't get stuck on yourself!*
> *Open up!"* [6]
> *Open up . . . Let go . . .*
> *Let go of the burden of self . . .*

Letting Go of the Bondage of Self

Harsh inner critics breed perpetual dissatisfaction with others as well as ourselves. Mindfulness practice helps us notice this. How often does your resting mind tilt toward nursing slights or feeding resentment? How often do we find ourselves chewing on the last time someone disappointed us or didn't live up to our standards? Research suggests that people who are compassionate toward themselves are more able to forgive others. They are happier, more resilient, and less self-concerned. They feel more a part of the larger universe of all beings.[7]

On one of my sojourns to study meditation in the East, I stayed at a guesthouse in Kathmandu, Nepal. I splurged on a higher-priced accommodation because the $3.00 a night room had a bathroom and the $1.50 a night room did not. Turns out it was a fortuitous choice because I got sick as a dog from bad *momos* (steamed dumplings filled with meat or vegetables) at the local restaurant. I had a funny feeling about the dumplings when I ate them and spent the next three days in bed, wishing I could call my mama to get comfort.

The guesthouse was down the street from the Boudhanath Stupa, a massive mound-like structure that contains Buddhist relics. Buddha-eyes are painted on each of the four sides of the structure—colorful, fierce, and omnipresent eyes. People in the area gather at dusk to circumambulate the stupa. Hundreds walked the path around the structure, praying with their mala beads and chanting the mantra of compassion. The ritual is beautiful.

After days of being sick in my room, I was lonely and my bones ached. Toward dusk, feeling a little better, I decided to wrap up in a woolen shawl and head out to the stupa. I joined in the flow of hundreds circling the sacred space, walking one step at a time and not going anywhere but around a circular path. It was as though my very skin absorbed the guttural, hypnotic tones of the Sanskrit chanting, despite not comprehending the literal words. I was held in the flow of the people's devotion, part of the great stream of all beings.

I wondered: *How many other people are sick from bad food today? Don't have food? Probably lots of people.*

The practice of circumambulating comforted me, lifting me out of the rumination that fed my dissatisfaction with myself, other people, and the world. Restored to the larger universe of all beings, my suffering lessened.

Try to notice the bondage of self and let go. Whatever other people do, it's not as much about *me* as it feels. Actually, not much that other people do *is* about us. Zen teacher Zoketsu Norman Fischer puts it like this: "Dealing with others is about *dealing with ourselves* dealing with others."[8] We're interpreting events and experiences and other people's actions through the lens of our internal formations, our stories about what's real. In fact, our inner critics live inside our personal *Truman Show* bubble much of the time. Those inner critics don't know we're inside the cocoon of our ego—our constructed reality, our *What-about-me?* place. Such concern with self is indeed a burden.

During one of my meditation intensives, a student wrote about the image that arose when he thought about being entrapped in the bondage of self: "It's like living inside a bubble. The parameters are limited because the bubble keeps other opportunities out. It's invisible, too, so you don't even know it's there. Once in a while you can see it."

I asked, "What is it like to be freed from the bubble of self?"

He replied: "It's like that joke about the Dalai Lama coming up to the hot dog stand to order. He says, 'I'll take one with every-thing.' All of a sudden you realize that you are just one little pixel on the TV screen of life. It's both scary and relieving. One day, I will fade away as soon as the power gets turned off, and that's just fine. That realization saves me from taking myself too seri-ously. While my sins are not unimportant, I am just a part of the culture—my family's culture, my society's culture, the world's culture—and I need to be forgiving of myself. Do my best and not take myself too seriously at the same time. It's not an either/ or proposition—it's both/and."

> There's only one point: "Don't get stuck on yourself!
>   Open up!"[9]
> Open up. Let go.
> Let go of the burden of self.

Founding members of the Twelve Step recovery program say that relief from the bondage of self is the path to recovery and inner healing. We could substitute "bondage of self" with "bondage of inner critics." They suggest we ask to be relieved of this burden in daily meditation and prayer, such as "Relieve me of the bondage of self, that I may better do [God's] will."[10] Dr. Bob, co-founder of Alcoholics Anonymous, used this as his personal prayer: "Please, God, move into my heart. However You do it is Your business, but make Yourself real inside me and fill my awful emptiness. Fill me with your love and Holy Spirit and [let me realize] Your will for me. . . ."[11]

This is a powerful practice—one we could consider making a part of our practice in releasing inner critics.

> *There's only one point: "Open up!"* [12]
> *To accept myself . . .*

Another prayer to free us from the bondage of self comes from Native American traditions. In the words of a Lakota Nation prayer known as Mitakuye Oyasin ("we are all related"):

> *Oh Great Spirit whose voice in the winds I hear,*
> *And whose breath gives life to all the world—*
> *Hear me. . . .*
> *I seek strength, not to be superior to [others],*
> *but to fight my greatest enemy—myself.*
> *Make me ready . . . So when life fades as the fading*
> *sunset, may my spirit stand before You*
> *without shame.* [13]

The Ease of Shamelessly Being Ourselves

What is it like to stand free, alive, flawed and yet free of shame?

On a spring morning in June, people filled every seat in the Bill Graham Civic Auditorium in San Francisco, California. All six thousand spaces held people waiting to hear the Dalai Lama and other Nobel laureates speak to the topic of "Peacemaking: The Power of Nonviolence." I was one of the minions.

Once a day, His Holiness gave a plenary session with lessons on peacemaking, forgiveness, and strategies for global rebuilding. A diminutive man, he walked on stage in the simple maroon and gold of a monk's garb—no fanfare, no confetti, no Gucci suit. He smiled, bobbed his head, and bowed to the crowd: first, to the hundreds of press flashing their bulbs, blinding his eyes; then to the rest of us, relishing his presence and waiting on his words. On the first day of the conference, His Holiness discussed inner peace. The next day, he talked about family peace. These sessions continued, building up to his final day's topic of global peacemaking through nonviolence.

The Dalai Lama used the same structure for each talk. After bowing to the audience, he would say, "I have three points" and then proceed.

On the fourth day, he began as usual: "I have three points." But this day, just as he got to his third point he paused.

We all waited. It was a long moment.

His Holiness was silent, frowning. At last he said, "What's my third point? I forgot my third point." He laughed with his whole body. *"I forgot my third point!"*

Then he looked at the hundreds of press gathered before him and said, "Humiliation" and laughed even more. He looked at the thousands of us in his audience and said again, *"Humiliation!"* He roared with mirth; tears ran down his cheeks. And we all rolled in the aisles with him. I laughed until my belly hurt.

A few moments later, as the merriment quelled, His Holiness pointed to his head, saying, "Oh, yes, now I remember!"

He went on to give an inspired talk, as if his temporary lapse was the most natural occurrence in the world. It was a moment of pure, ego-less connection to his audience.

I've never forgotten the ease of his freedom and joy—shamelessly being himself, without exception. In his place, I would have wanted to fall through the floor.

People in long-term recovery from addictions, co-dependency, or harsh inner critics describe a similar loosening and letting go of the preoccupation with self. They have greater comfort in their skin, an easier breath, and more gentleness toward themselves and others about their shortcomings.

> *There's only one point:*
> *"Let go of holding on to yourself . . ."* [14]
> *Let go . . . Open up! . . .*

Remembering Our True Face

Great spiritual teachers say that after years of meditation they experience a dropping away of body and mind—conscious contact with the Great Reality within. Buddhists refer to this spiritual awakening as "remembering our original face."

Some writers liken spiritual development to a sculptor creating a beautiful piece of work. The artist chisels away the stone that is not a part of his or her creation. The excess falls away to reveal a masterpiece. So, too, in mindfulness and meditation practice, we allow the overlays of our conditioning, stories, and mental formations held by our inner critics to fall away. Our original, true face is then revealed.

This is a gentle approach—an opening of the doors and windows of our ego-constructed house and letting the air out of our *Truman Show* bubble of self. With kindness. At our own pace. With the help of others. With prayer and meditation as our guides.

Ancient teachings by Zen master Dōgen Zenji[15] say that this letting go of self is "the fundamental point" to mindfulness and spiritual practice. In his renowned teaching, the *Gengo-koan*,[16] he says in verse 4:

> *To study the [Path of awakening] is to study the self.*
> *To study the self is to forget the self.*
> *To forget the self is to be actualized by myriad things.*
> *When actualized by myriad things, your body and mind*
>   *as well as the bodies and minds of others drop away.*
> *... The moment [you see this truth], you are*
>   *immediately your original self.*[17]

> *There is only one point.*
> *This is the one point . . .*
> *Open up!*

Letting Go of Self: Opening Up!

Here are some simple (but not easy) practices for helping us to open up!

Try This:

1. *Take three breaths to break the chain reaction of old mental and emotional habits:*[18]

   - Notice when habitual negative thinking arises.

   - Stop. Literally stop for a moment: If you are walking, stop walking; if you are sitting, stand up; if you are thinking, stop thinking.

   - Take a breath. Return to awareness with that breath.

2. *Think of others.* Do something to make another person happy, preferably anonymously, even something small. This practice can get you out of yourself and connected with others and help you feel less alone in your struggles: *Can I serve? Am I less preoccupied with myself and more available to others than I used to be?*[19]

3. *Turn your mind to another "channel," similar to when you switch channels on the radio from AM to FM.* Use your training in mindfulness to choose the focus of your attention— switching from critical, self-referential thoughts to practicing gratitude (such as Naikan practice[20]), or reciting loving-kindness phrases, or repeating a favorite passage from scripture, or reading aloud a beautiful piece of poetry that touches you. Mental recitation of this kind etches new neural pathways in the brain, bumps our busy neurons from the well-worn path of our established mental habits to a newer pathway. (This technique brings to mind another *lojong* slogan: *If you can practice even when distracted, you are well-trained.*)

4. *Write a compassionate letter to yourself every day for seven days.* Take care to hold an attitude of "I care about your pain" toward yourself, considering the causes and conditions that led you to act however you did. This is not to be confused with excusing yourself or not taking responsibility for your actions or excusing yourself for bad behavior. In fact, research on self-compassion suggests that self-compassion increases people's ability to take responsibility for their actions even when they're bad—and accepting ourselves as human.[21]

5. *"Act as if" with kindness—even if you don't feel like it.* Acting as if is a tried-and-true strategy of people in recovery and strongly recommended by Alcoholics Anonymous and Al-Anon. In this case, practice acting as if you feel kindness toward yourself or another person about whom you have critical thoughts or feelings.

6. *Return to the fundamental mindfulness practice of breathing and noting.* Take special notice of the me-based stories running through your mind, such as *poor me, why me,* or *woe is me.* Practice creating spaciousness and dis-identifying with these stories. Let them go through the mind rather than feed them with your attention.

There is only one point.

Be awakened by myriad things . . . Let concern with
  the self drop away . . .

So you can love others . . .

My granddaughters' beautiful faces . . .

The warmth of Jim's touch when he holds my hand . . .

The sensation of my heart beating . . .

The sound of Kukla's purring as she curls in my lap . . .

The smell of morning tea . . .

The blood moon in the night sky . . .

The "Great We" of fellowship and humankind . . .

The spaciousness of mind . . .

A few years back, while at lush Green Gulch Farm Zen Center in California, I attended a workshop led by Myogen Steve Stücky, then head abbot of the center. A grounded, down-to-earth presence (but sadly now deceased), he said, "If you have no other meditation practice, do this: Each morning when you get out of bed, before your feet touch the floor, ask yourself this: *What is the most important thing?*"

CHAPTER 6

There is only one thing . . .
Only one point . . .
One . . .

In the end these things matter most:
How well did you love?
How fully did you live?
How deeply did you let go?

—Gautama Buddha

❖

Basic Meditation Instructions

Mindfulness Meditation

- *Notice your breathing.* Come in to the present moment by simply noticing the sensations associated with inhaling and exhaling. Don't try to change the rhythm of your breathing. Just let it happen and rest your attention there.

- *As thoughts arise, let them go.* There's no need to engage with thoughts in any way—no need to elaborate on them, judge them, or stop them. Simply be aware of thoughts and surrender any control over them. Let them arise and pass away on their own.

- *Become aware of other sensations.* After a few moments of breath meditation, open up to sounds, sights, aromas, tastes, or sensations in other parts of the body. *Any* object of attention can bring you into the present moment. Again, if thoughts arise, simply notice them and let them go.

Loving-Kindness Meditation

- *Bring yourself to the present moment.* Take a few deep breaths. Rest your attention on any prominent sensation associated with breathing.

- *Fill yourself with warmth and compassion.* Imagine your chest glowing with light and energy as you repeat the following words of loving-kindness:

  May I feel safe,
  May I be happy,
  May I be healthy,
  May I live with ease.

Do this for a minute or two . . . or three . . . or four.

- *Extend this field of loving energy to include someone you care about.* Repeat the loving-kindness words for this person—for example:

  May my mother feel safe,
  May my mother be happy,
  May my mother be healthy,
  May my mother live with ease.

- *Now, extend the field of loving energy to include a neutral person.* This can be anyone for whom you feel no particular attraction or aversion. Repeat the loving-kindness words for this person—for example:

  May the mail carrier feel safe,
  May the mail carrier be happy,
  May the mail carrier be healthy,
  May the mail carrier live with ease.

- *Next, extend the field of energy to someone you dislike.* Again, modify the words of loving-kindness to embrace this person—for example:

  May my supervisor feel safe,
  May my supervisor be happy,
  May my supervisor be healthy,
  May my supervisor live with ease.

- *Finally, imagine the field of energy enlarging to include the rest of the world.* Visualize all people, animals, and the natural world dwelling in the kind light of compassion.

To deepen your practice of loving-kindness meditation, increase the amount of time that you spend on each of the above steps.

❖

A Few Words about
"Third Wave" Therapies

In 2004, Dr. Steven Hayes, professor of psychology at the University of Nevada, coined the term *third wave therapies* for relatively new mindfulness-based practices for working with inner critics.[1] Hayes distinguished these practices from the "first wave" of behavior therapy and the "second wave" of cognitive therapy, which also includes cognitive-behavioral therapy (CBT).

According to Hayes, CBT aims to change the *content* of thinking by replacing distressing, irrational thoughts with stress-reducing, rational thoughts. The premise—actually quite Eastern in nature—is that our emotions are not determined by any external situation. Rather, emotions flow from our thoughts *about* a situation, or about ourselves in that situation.

To help people replace irrational thoughts, a CBT therapist might ask, *What is going through your mind right now? Are these thoughts accurate or do they reflect a negative, self-critical mental habit?* Once we rout out the distortions in our thinking—largely by disputing our negative thoughts and learning to think and act more realistically—we are supposed to feel better. And, many people do.

In contrast, mindfulness-based therapies work with the *process* of thinking. Instead of routing out irrational thoughts and replacing them with new ones, people learn to change their *relationship* with any stream of thought that enters their minds.[2] Here the aim of treatment is to distinguish our interpretations of events ("stories") from the verifiable facts about those events. We stop identifying with our stories, stop judging thoughts, and stop engaging with our mental distortions. Mindfulness is a tool for doing this. To this process, we add a big dollop of self-compassion as well.

The idea behind a third wave therapy called compassion-focused therapy (CFT) is to take the strengths of CBT treatments and "warm them up." Psychologist Paul Gilbert, author of *The Compassionate Mind,* says that "survivors of childhood maltreatment can readily identify their maladaptive thought patterns ('I'm unlovable') and provide alternative self-statements ('Some people love me'), but they do not necessarily find cognitive restructuring emotionally reassuring."[3] In order to heal our inner critics, we need to do more than change the structure of our thoughts. We need to build a kinder voice. We need to give ourselves the caring we lack.

Third wave mindfulness-based therapies are helpful in treating depression, anxiety, posttraumatic stress, and a host of other mental health conditions. Research indicates that these therapies are also effective for relapse prevention with people in recovery.

In general, third wave therapies foster greater happiness for people with a variety of mental health diagnoses. In fact, a recent study by the Veterans Administration in Minneapolis found that veterans engaged in mindfulness training showed a more rapid decline in the severity of their posttraumatic stress symptoms than a comparison group who received standard group therapy. And, these results were obtained after only nine weeks of training! Melissa Polusny, a psychologist who co-authored the study, notes that "mindfulness training reflects a growing wave of alternative therapies in mainstream medicine."[4]

This point of view is supported by the work of Dr. Richard Davidson at the University of Wisconsin. He found that mindfulness training leads to structural and functional changes in the brain (changes in the way the brain looks as well as how it operates). Davidson adds that these "aren't just changes during the meditation state itself, but they're changes that persist beyond the meditation state. They transform our baseline."[5]

In short, the mind-training practices presented in this book lie at the exciting intersection of ancient meditation teachings and modern science. We can combine the best from both of these worlds to release the suffering that originates in the voices of our inner critics.

Notes

Dedication

1. These phrases are from Buddhist loving-kindness meditation ("metta meditation"), adapted from Sharon Salzberg (Insight Meditation Society, Barre, Massachusetts) and Sylvia Boorstein (Spirit Rock Meditation Center, San Francisco, California).

Introduction: Always Train with Slogans

1. The Ignation Exercises are a compilation of meditations, prayers, and contemplative practices developed by St. Ignatius Loyola (composed 1522–1524) to help people deepen their relationship with God. For centuries the Exercises were most commonly given as a "long retreat" of about thirty days in solitude and silence. In recent years, the most common way of going through the Exercises is a "retreat in daily life," which involves a month-long program of daily prayer and meetings with a spiritual director.

2. The Spiritual Life Institute's original monastery, Nada Hermitage in Sedona, Arizona (1963–1983) was lost to land development in 1983, at which time Nada Hermitage moved to Crestone, Colorado.

3. Bengali teacher Atisha is said to have introduced mind-training slogans in 982.

4. Norman Fischer, "Abandon Hope and Other Surprising Slogans to Help You Handle Anger," *Shambhala Sun Magazine,* September 2014.

5. Norman Fischer, *Training in Compassion: Zen Teachings on the Practice of Lojong* (Boston: Shambhala Publications, 2012), xvii.

6. Ibid.

7. Slogan practice (*lojong*) is combined with a compassion breath practice called *tonglen* in traditional Tibetan mind-training.

8. The "we version" of the Serenity Prayer is as follows:

> *God, grant us the serenity*
> *to accept the things we cannot change,*
> *courage to change the things we can,*
> *and wisdom to know the difference.*

9. Norman Fischer, "Abandon Hope and Other Surprising Slogans to Help You Handle Anger," *Shambhala Sun Magazine,* September 2014.

10. Chögyam Trungpa, *Training the Mind and Cultivating Loving-Kindness,* edited by Judith L. Lief (Boston: Shambhala Publications, 1993), editor's forward.

11. Adapted from Norman Fischer, *Training in Compassion: Zen Teachings on the Practice of Lojong* (Boston: Shambhala Publications, 2012), xvii.

12. Ibid.

13. Ibid.

Chapter 1: Everything Is of the Nature to Change (Even Us)

1. Phrase attributed to Carla J. Shatz, an American neurobiologist, as cited in Rick Hanson, *Buddha's Brain: The Practical Neuroscience of Happiness, Love, and Wisdom* (Oakland, CA: New Harbinger Publications, 2009), referenced as the "Hebbian theory," Hebb 1949; LeDoux 2003, 33.

   Neuroscientists like Joseph LeDoux and Gerald Edelman have advanced the theory that "neurons that fire together wire together." This means that when a group of neurons is activated by the "firing" of an electrochemical signal across their synapses, this produces changes that "wire" the neurons together in a closer grouping by increasing the number and efficiency of synaptic ties between those neurons.

2. W. Cunningham and P. D. Zelazo, "Attitudes and Evaluations: A Social Cognitive Perspective," *Trends in Cognitive Sciences* 11 (2007): 97–104, cited in Rick Hanson, *Buddha's Brain: The Practical Neuroscience of Happiness, Love, and Wisdom* (Oakland, CA: New Harbinger Publications, 2009), 33.

3. Richard Davidson is a professor of psychology and psychiatry at the University of Wisconsin–Madison and chair of the Center for Investigating Healthy Minds at the Waisman Center.

4. Sara Lazar, the study's senior author, is a researcher in the Massachusetts General Hospital (MGH) Psychiatric Neuroimaging Research Program and a Harvard Medical School instructor in psychology.

    From "7 Ways Meditation Can Actually Change the Brain," by Alice G. Walton, *Forbes,* February 9, 2015:

    Eight weeks of Mindfulness-Based Stress Reduction (MBSR) was found to increase cortical thickness in the hippocampus, which governs learning and memory, and in certain areas of the brain that play roles in emotion regulation and self-referential processing. There were also *decreases* in brain cell volume in the amygdala, which is responsible for fear, anxiety, and stress—and these changes matched the participants' self-reports of their stress levels, indicating that meditation not only changes the brain, but it changes our subjective perception and feelings as well.

5. Chanting, mantras, music, guided imagery, or yoga practices were not considered in this study. Lazar et al. say, "Other forms of yoga and meditation will likely have a similar impact on cortical structure, although each tradition would be expected to have a slightly different pattern of cortical thickening based on the specific mental exercises involved."

6. From *The Washington Post,* May 26, 2015, in the *Inspired Life* column by Brigid Schulte, "Harvard Neuroscientist: Meditation Not Only Reduces Stress, Here's How It Changes Your Brain," http://www .washingtonpost.com/news/inspired-life/wp/2015/05/26/harvard-neuroscientist-meditation-not-only-reduces-stress-it-literally-changes-your-brain.

    Specifically, the areas of the brain that Lazar and her team found are:

    • Involved in mind wandering and self-relevance (the posterior cingulate).

    • Assist in learning, cognition, memory and emotional regulation (the left hippocampus).

- Associated with perspective taking, empathy and compassion (the temporo parietal junction, or TPJ).

- Produce regulatory neurotransmitters (an area of the brain stem called the Pons).

7. S. W. Lazar, C. E. Kerr, R. H. Wasserman, J. R. Gray, D. N. Greve, M. T. Treadway, M. McGarvey, B. T. Quinn, J. A. Dusek, H. Benson, S. L. Rauch, C. L. Moore, and B. Fischl, "Meditation Experience Is Associated with Increased Cortical Thickness," *Neuroreport* 16, no. 17 (2005): 1893–7.

8. Richard Davidson quoted in "Meditation Gives Brain a Charge, Study Finds" by Marc Kaufman, *Washington Post,* January 3, 2005, http://www.washingtonpost.com/wp-dyn/articles/A43006-2005Jan2.html.

9. Richard Davidson quoted in "Neuroscientist Richard Davidson on How Happiness Can Be Learned," by Lindsay Holmes, *The Huffington Post,* January 23, 2015.

10. Richard Davidson and Antoine Lutz, "Buddha's Brain: Neuroplasticity and Meditation," published in final edited form as *IEEE Signal Processing Magazine* 25, no. 1 (January 2008): 176–74.

Chapter 2: Rest in the Openness of Mind

1. "The genesis of *The Truman Show* was a spec script by [Andrew] Niccol, inspired by an episode of *The Twilight Zone* called 'Special Service.' Scott Rudin purchased the script, and immediately set the project up at Paramount Pictures. . . . The film was a financial and critical success, and earned numerous nominations at the 71st Academy Awards, 56th Golden Globe Awards, 52nd British Academy Film Awards and The Saturn Awards." Source: "*The Truman Show,*" Wikipedia, accessed November 27, 2015.

2. Barbara Hoetsu O'Brien, "Dependent Origination: 'When This Is, That Is,'" at http://buddhism.about.com/od/basicbuddhistteachings/a/genesis.htm. Ms. O'Brien is a journalist and student of Zen Buddhism currently residing in the Zen Center of New York City in Brooklyn.

3. Richard Conn Henry, "The Mental Universe," *Nature* 436, no. 29 (July 2005).

4. Immanuel Kant (1724–1804) was a German philosopher, considered to be the central figure of modern philosophy.

5. Mindfulness-based stress reduction (MBSR), developed by Jon Kabat-Zinn at the University of Massachusetts General Hospital, is a mindfulness-based program designed to assist people with pain and a range of conditions and life issues that were initially difficult to treat in a hospital setting.

6. Thích Nhất Hạnh, quoting Buddha, http://www.livinglifefully.com /thinkershanh.htm.

7. Ronald Potter-Efron and Patricia Potter-Efron, *Letting Go of Shame: Understanding How Shame Affects Your Life* (Center City, MN: Hazelden, 1989), 14.

8. Buddhist definition of "suchness" is "reality in its ultimate nature."

9. "Yongey Mingyur Rinpoche is a Nepalese teacher and master of the Karma Kagyu and Nyingma lineages of Tibetan Buddhism. He has authored two best-selling books and oversees the Tergar Meditation Community, a global network of Buddhist meditation centers." Source: "Yongey Mingyur Rinpoche," Wikipedia, accessed November 26, 2015.

10. Despite the many controversies surrounding Chögyam Trungpa, he remains one of the foremost meditation teachers to bring *lojong* slogan practice to the West, and was the venerable Pema Chödrön's teacher. Chögyam Trungpa, *Training the Mind and Cultivating Loving-Kindness,* edited by Judith L. Lief (Boston: Shambhala Publications, 1993), 21.

Chapter 3: Stay Close (and Do Nothing)

1. The forty-second Zen ancestor was Liangshan Yuanguan (Chinese: 梁山緣觀; Japanese: Ryozan Enkan) as cited in "Beginner's Mind" by Abbess Zenkei Blanche Hartman of the San Francisco Zen Center, http://www.chzc.org/hartman4.htm.

2. The forty-first Zen ancestor was Tongan Guanzhi (Chinese: 同安觀志; Japanese: Dōan Kanshi) as cited in ibid.

3. Literal translation of the Zen story says, "What is the matter under this robe?"

4. Norman Fischer, *Training in Compassion: Zen Teachings on the Practice of Lojong* (Boston: Shambhala Publications, 2012), 138.

5. *Acharya* is a Sanskrit word referring to a highly learned teacher.

6. Stephen Brammeier, Jan Brennan, Sondra Brown et al., "Good Trainers: How to Identify One . . . ," *Journal of Veterinary Behavior* 1 (2006): 47–52. This article recommends dog-friendly dog training with your dog. Read more at https://positively.com/contributors/being-nice-to-your-dog-is-good-science/#sthash.0FqsZDF5.dpuf.

7. Richard Schwartz, *Introduction to the Internal Family Systems Model* (Oak Park: Trailheads Publications, 2001). The internal family systems (IFS) model represents a synthesis of two already-existing psychotherapeutic paradigms: systems thinking and the multiplicity of the mind. IFS integrates concepts and methods from the structural, strategic, narrative, and Bowenian schools of family therapy.

8. Ibid., reference to Thomas Keating, 35.

9. Morgen E. Peck, "Harsh, Critical Parenting May Lead to Anxiety Disorder Symptoms: 'Tiger' Parents May Drive Kids' Brains to Overreact to Errors," *Scientific American,* April 9, 2015.

10. Paraphrased from a talk by Thích Nhất Hạnh at Plum Village, "Mara and the Buddha–Embracing Our Suffering," August 4, 2013, http://plumvillage.org/transcriptions/mara-and-the-buddha-embracing-our-suffering. Plum Village is the spiritual community in France founded by Thích Nhất Hạnh.

11. Thích Nhất Hạnh, *Peace Is Every Step: The Path of Mindfulness in Everyday Life* (New York: Bantam Books, 1991), 53.

12. Richard Schwartz, *Introduction to the Internal Family Systems Model* (Oak Park: Trailheads Publications, 2001), 73.

13. These questions are adapted from Schwartz, ibid.

14. Jay Earley and Bonnie Weiss, *Freedom from Your Inner Critic: A Self-Therapy Approach* (Louisville, CO: Sounds True, 2013).

15. Donald E. Kalsched and Daniela F. Sieff, "Uncovering the Secrets of the Traumatised Psyche," in *Understanding and Healing Emotional Trauma: Conversations with Pioneering Clinicians and Researchers,* by Daniela F. Sieff (London: Routledge, 2015), 11.

16. Ibid.

17. Pema Chödrön, "Learning to Stay," chap. 4 in *The Places That Scare You: A Guide to Fearlessness in Difficult Times* (Boston: Shambhala Publications, 2002), 25.

18. Kristin Neff, *Self-Compassion: The Proven Power of Being Kind to Yourself* (New York: William Morrow, 2015).

19. From the Christian hymn of the same name, 1845.

20. Carl Rogers, *On Becoming a Person: A Therapist's View of Psychotherapy* (New York: Mariner Books, 1995), 17.

21. A mudrā is a ritual gesture or "hand prayer" in Hinduism and Buddhism. While some mudrās involve the entire body, most are performed with the hands and fingers.

22. Kristin Neff and Katie Dahm, "Self-Compassion: What It Is, What It Does, and How It Relates to Mindfulness," to appear in *Mindfulness and Self-Regulation,* edited by M. Robinson, B. Meier, and B. Ostafin (New York: Springer, 2016).

Chapter 4: Train in the Three Difficulties

1. The Presidential Youth Fitness Program replaced the Presidential Physical Fitness Test in 2012.

2. From Alice Park, "Is It Genes, or the Gym, That Makes Great Athletes? Q&A with Author of *The Sports Gene* [David Epstein]," *Time Magazine,* August 14, 2013.

3. The 10,000-hour theory has its origins in a 1993 study by Anders Ericsson, where he looked at the performance ability of violinists, and showed that the playing ability was determined by the cumulative hours of training up to the age of twenty.

4. From an interview with Matthieu Ricard where he quotes the Dalai Lama, as cited in "Why You Shun Enlightenment," by William Berry, *Psychology Today,* October 25, 2015, https://www.psychologytoday .com/blog/the-second-noble-truth/201510/why-you-shun-enlighten- ment.

5. Matthieu Ricard quoting the Dalai Lama in ideas.ted.com/want-to- be-happy-slow-down.

6. A phrase used by Tara Brach, author of *Radical Acceptance,* when describing the "trance of unworthiness" in a dharma talk at the Insight Meditation Center on August 8, 2012; available in her collection of Real But Not True audio talks at http://www.tarabrach.com/real-but- not-true-audio.

7. From commentary on the second difficulty in *The Great Path of Awak- ening: An Easily Accessible Introduction for Ordinary People* by Jamgon Kongtrul, translated by Ken McLeod (Boston: Shambhala Classics, 2005), as seen on http://lojongmindtraining.com/Commentary.aspx?- author=4&proverb=42.

Lojongmindtraining.com is an online database of commentaries on the Tibetan Buddhist meditation practices of *lojong* (mind training) and *tonglen* (compassion breathing). On this site, the *lojong* slogan "Train in the Three Difficulties" is translated as "Recognize Your Neurotic Tendencies, Overcome Them, Then Transcend Them."

8. Pico Iyer, *The Art of Stillness: Adventures in Going Nowhere* (New York: Simon & Schuster, 2014), 13.

9. The Third Step of Alcoholics Anonymous is "Made a decision to turn our will and our lives over to the care of God *as we understood [God].*"

10. Pema Chödrön's commentary on the slogan "Train in the Three Diffi- culties," as found on www.lojongmindtraining.com.

11. "Pause Practice" is a term coined by meditation teacher Pema Chödrön.

12. Thérèse Jacobs-Stewart, *Paths Are Made by Walking: Practical Steps for Attaining Serenity* (New York: Time Warner, 2003), 35.

13. If you are interested in further exploring disputing mental thoughts, look to the literature on cognitive restructuring used in cognitive-behavioral therapy (CBT). I recommend David Burns, *Feeling Good: The New Mood Therapy* (Paperback edition, 2008; Kindle edition, 2012) as a good introductory read.

14. Reference to research on Irish family systems as reported by Monica McGoldrick in *Ethnicity and Family Therapy,* 3rd ed. (New York: Guilford Press, 2005).

15. Christopher Germer and Kristin Neff, "Cultivating Self-Compassion in Trauma Survivors," in *Mindfulness-Oriented Interventions for Trauma: Integrating Contemplative Practices,* edited by Victoria Follette et al. (New York: Guilford Press, 2015), 43–44.

16. Ibid., 44.

17. Ibid., 46.

Chapter 5: Begin Kindness Practice with Yourself

1. The story of King Pasenadi and Queen Mallikā is reported in Bhikkhu Thanissaro's translation of the Udana in the Buddhist Pali canon, Ud 5.1 PTS: Ud 47, *Rājan Sutta: The King.*

2. Yongey Mingyur Rinpoche, in a lecture at the University of Minnesota, 2009, described using mental recitation as in meditation as "giving the monkey-mind—the unsettled, restless mind—a job."

3. Kristin Neff, "The Physiology of Self-Compassion," http://self-compassion.org/the-physiology-of-self-compassion.

4. Sharon Salzberg, *Loving-Kindness: The Revolutionary Art of Happiness* (Boston: Shambhala Publications, 1995). Salzberg cites the Buddha as saying that the intimacy and caring that fill our hearts as the force of loving-kindness develops will bring eleven particular advantages:

(1) You will sleep easily. (2) You will wake easily. (3) You will have pleasant dreams. (4) People will love you. (5) Devas [celestial beings] and animals will love you. (6) Devas will protect you. (7) External dangers [poisons, weapons, and fire] will not harm you. (8) Your face will be radiant. (9) Your mind will be serene. (10) You will die unconfused.

(11) You will be reborn in happy realms.

5. Nyanaponika Thera or Nyanaponika Mahathera (1901–1994) was a German-born Sri-Lanka-ordained Theravada monk, co-founder of the Buddhist Publication Society, contemporary author of numerous seminal Theravada books, and teacher of contemporary Western Buddhist leaders such as Bhikkhu Bodhi.

6. Nyanaponika Mahathera, "The Four Sublime States: Contemplations on Love, Compassion, Sympathetic Joy and Equanimity," *Access to Insight (Legacy Edition)*, November 30, 2013, http://www.accesstoinsight.org/lib/authors/nyanaponika/wheel006.html.

7. Ibid.

8. Ibid.

9. Thích Nhất Hạnh, "The Buddha's Love," *Shambhala Sun Magazine*, January 2015.

10. Loving-kindness ("metta") phrases originated as "The Four Limitless Ones" chant offered by Shantideva in *Bodhicharyavatara: A Guide to the Bodhisattva's Way of Life*, translated here by the venerable Pema Chödrön:

    May I (we) enjoy happiness and the root of happiness.
    May I (we) be free from suffering and the root of suffering.
    May I (we) not be separated from the great happiness devoid of suffering.
    May I (we) dwell in the great equanimity free from passion, aggression, and prejudice.

11. This translation of the loving-kindness aspirations is from Sharon Salzberg, *Loving-Kindness: The Revolutionary Art of Happiness* (Boston: Shambhala Publications, 1995).

12. Pema Chödrön, *Start Where You Are: A Guide to Compassionate Living* (Boston: Shambhala Publications, 1994), 88–89.

Chapter 6: There's Only One Point

1. Pema Chödrön, *Start Where You Are: A Guide to Compassionate Living* (Boston: Shambhala Publications, 1994), 88–89.

2. C. L. Aberson, M. Healy, and V. Romero, "Ingroup Bias and Self-Esteem: A Meta-Analysis," *Personality and Social Psychology Review* 4 (2000): 157–173; C. C. Morf and F. Rhodewalt, "Unraveling the Paradoxes of Narcissism: A Dynamic Self-Regulatory Processing Model," *Psychological Inquiry* 12 (2001): 177–196; C. Salmivalli, A. Kaukiainen, L. Kaistaniemi, and K. M. J. Lagerspetz, "Self-Evaluated Self-Esteem, Peer-Evaluated Self-Esteem, and Defensive Egotism as Predictors of Adolescents' Participation in Bullying Situations," *Personality and Social Psychology Bulletin* 25 (1999): 1268–1278; all cited in Kristin Neff and Katie Dahm, "Self-Compassion: What It Is, What It Does, and How It Relates to Mindfulness," to appear in *Mindfulness and Self-Regulation,* edited by M. Robinson, B. Meier, and B. Ostafin (New York: Springer, 2016), found at www.self-compassion.org.

3. Kristin Neff, *Self-Compassion: The Proven Power of Being Kind to Yourself* (New York: William Morrow, 2015).

4. From teaching by His Holiness the Dalai Lama at *Generating the Mind of Enlightenment,* Washington, New Jersey, May 7, 1998, cited at http://www.lamayeshe.com/article/generating-mind-enlightenment. His Holiness is quoting from a symposium he had participated in at Beth Israel Medical Center's Institute for Neurology and Neurosurgery (INN), May 1998.

5. Study by Kristin Neff, Kristin Kirkpatrick, and Stephanie Rude (2007), as cited in the *Handbook of Individual Differences in Social Behavior,* edited by Mark R. Leary and Rick H. Hoyle (New York: Guilford Press, 2009), 563.

6. Norman Fischer, *Training in Compassion: Zen Teachings on the Practice of Lojong* (Boston: Shambhala Publications, 2012), 82.

7. Kristin Neff and Katie Dahm, "Self-Compassion: What It Is, What It Does, and How It Relates to Mindfulness," to appear in *Mindfulness and Self-Regulation,* edited by M. Robinson, B. Meier, and B. Ostafin (eds.) (New York: Springer, 2016).

8. Norman Fischer, *Training in Compassion: Zen Teachings on the Practice of Lojong* (Boston: Shambhala Publications, 2012), 97.

9. Ibid., 82.

10. Third Step Prayer, *Alcoholics Anonymous*, 4th ed. (New York: Alcoholics Anonymous World Services, 2001), 63.

11. Third Step Prayer used by Dr. Bob, cofounder of the Twelve Step program of Alcoholics Anonymous, www.greenbayaa.org/pdf/aaprayers /stepthree.pdf.

12. Norman Fischer, *Training in Compassion: Zen Teachings on the Practice of Lojong* (Boston: Shambhala Publications, 2012), 82.

13. Native American Third Step Prayer from www.greenbayaa.org/pdf /aaprayers/stepthree. Aho Mitakuye Oyasin is a simple (yet profound) statement spoken during prayer and ceremonies in the Lakota Nation to invite and acknowledge all relatives to the moment. This version is offered as an alternate Third Step prayer by an AA group in Green Bay, WI, found at http://www.greenbayaa.org/pdf/aaprayers/stepthree.pdf.

14. From commentary on the *lojong* slogan "There's Only One Point" by Pema Chödrön in *Start Where You Are: A Guide to Compassionate Living* (Boston: Shambhala Publications, 1994), 88–89, as seen on http:// lojongmindtraining.com/Commentary.aspx?author=3&proverb=17. Pema translates this *lojong* slogan as "All dharma ['truth'] agrees at one point."

15. Dōgen Zenji (1200–1253) was a Japanese Zen Buddhist teacher born in Kyōto. He founded the Sōtō school of Zen in Japan after travelling to China and training under Tiāntóng Rújìng, a master of the Chinese Caodong lineage.

16. "Actualizing the Fundamental Point" (*Gengo-koan*), trans. Robert Aitken and Kazuaki Tanahashi. Revised at San Francisco Zen Center and later at Berkeley Zen Center; published in Tanahashi, *Enlightenment Unfolds: The Essential Teachings of Zen Master Dōgen* (Boston: Shambhala Publications, 2000), 35–39, from http://www.thezensite .com/ZenTeachings/Dogen_Teachings/GenjoKoan8.htm.

17. Ibid. The full translation of verse 4 of the *Gengo-koan* is as follows:

To study the buddha way is to study the self. To study the self is to forget the self. To forget the self is to be actualized by myriad things. When actualized by myriad things, your body and mind as well as the bodies and minds of others drop away. No trace of realization remains, and this no-trace continues endlessly. When you first seek dharma, you imagine you are far away from its environs. At the moment when dharma is correctly transmitted, you are immediately your original self.

18. These suggestions are adapted from the teachings of Norman Fischer.

19. Ibid. Fischer-roshi says asking the question "Am I less stuck on myself, more available to others than I used to be?" is a good way to assess your spiritual practice and offers important information. If your answer is no, Fischer-roshi says, "You know what you have to do. Invite someone out to lunch. Ask someone how she is. Practice more loving-kindness and *tonglen*."

20. Naikan is a Japanese word meaning "inside looking" or "introspection." It is a structured method of self-reflection developed by Yoshimoto Ishin, a devout Buddhist of the Jodo Shinshu sect in Japan. Naikan practice has been introduced to the West by Gregg Krech in his beautiful book *Naikan: Gratitude, Grace, and the Japanese Art of Self-Reflection* (Berkeley, CA: Stone Bridge Press, 2002).

21. This practice is referenced in the research on self-compassion reported by Kristin Neff, *Self-Compassion: The Proven Power of Being Kind to Yourself* (New York: William Morrow, 2015).

Appendix 2: A Few Words about "Third Wave" Therapies

1. Steven C. Hayes is known for relational frame theory and its application to various psychological difficulties, as seen in his work on Acceptance and Commitment Therapy (ACT). In 1992, the Institute for Scientific Information cited Dr. Hayes as the thirtieth "highest impact" psychologist in the world during 1986–1990.

2. From S. C. Hayes, "Acceptance and Commitment Therapy, Relational Frame Theory, and the Third Wave of Behavior Therapy," in *Behavior Therapy* 35 (2004): 639–65, as cited by Brian Thompson in "Investigating the Similarities and Differences Between Practitioners of Second- and Third-Wave Cognitive Behavioral Therapies," in *Scientific Mindfulness* post, March 3, 2011, http://www.scientificmindfulness .com/2011/03/investigating-similarities-and.html.

3. Christopher Germer and Kristin Neff, "Cultivating Self-Compassion in Trauma Survivors," in *Mindfulness-Oriented Interventions for Trauma:*

Integrating Contemplative Practices, edited by Victoria Follette et al. (New York: Guilford Press, 2015), 46.

4. Jeremy Olson, "Meditation Calms Minnesota Vets Struggling with PTSD, Study by VA Finds," *Star Tribune,* August 4, 2015.

5. Mandy Oaklander, "Bounce Back: Scientists Now Know Why Some People Rebound So Well from Setbacks," *Time Magazine,* June 1, 2015, 26–30. This article notes the role meditation can have on fostering brain resiliency.

About the Author

Thérèse Jacobs-Stewart, a licensed psychotherapist for more than thirty-five years, was among the pioneers in recognizing the similarity between Twelve Step recovery programs and the ancient Buddhist path of mindfulness. Her books integrate meditative practices with the latest research in psychology and neuroscience, offering new insights into what it means to live fully—body, mind, and spirit—in the here and now. A noted lecturer and retreat leader, Thérèse is a recognized expert in contemplative meditation techniques and compassion-based cognitive psychotherapy and is the author of *Paths Are Made by Walking: Practical Steps for Attaining Serenity* (2003) and *Mindfulness and the 12 Steps* (2010).

About Hazelden Publishing

As part of the Hazelden Betty Ford Foundation, Hazelden Publishing offers both cutting-edge educational resources and inspirational books. Our print and digital works help guide individuals in treatment and recovery, and their loved ones. Professionals who work to prevent and treat addiction also turn to Hazelden Publishing for evidence-based curricula, digital content solutions, and videos for use in schools, treatment programs, correctional programs, and electronic health records systems. We also offer training for implementation of our curricula.

Through published and digital works, Hazelden Publishing extends the reach of healing and hope to individuals, families, and communities affected by addiction and related issues.

For more information about Hazelden publications,
please call **800-328-9000**
or visit us online at **hazelden.org/bookstore.**